# Essential Skills
## for Papua New Guinea

# Spelling

GRADE 5

Peter Durkin

OXFORD

Oxford University Press is a department of the University of Oxford.

It furthers the University's objective of excellence in research, scholarship, and education by publishing worldwide. Oxford is a registered trademark of Oxford University Press in the UK and in certain other countries.

Published in Australia by
Oxford University Press
253 Normanby Road, South Melbourne, Victoria 3205, Australia



First published 2013
Reprinted 2022(D)



ISBN 978 0 19551843 6



Edited by Emma Short
Cover design by Sarah Hazell
Text design by Sarah Hazell
Typeset by Sarah Hazell
Illustrations by Birdwing Group
Printed and bound in Australia by Ligare Book Printers Pty Ltd

# To the Student ›

## This book will help you learn about spelling. You will learn:

How two-letter patterns can make the same sound, for example:

- meat
- meet

How different letters can make the same sound, for example:

- sun
- circle

How to spell words with silent letters, for example:

- silent '**k**' as in '**knife**'
- silent '**w**' as in '**write**'

You will also learn some 'common words'.
They are important because you use them in your writing.
Some common words are difficult to sound out, so you need to practise spelling them every day.

Some examples of common words are:

- favourite → My **favourite** colour is green.
- finished → Have you **finished** your homework yet?
- coming → Are you **coming** to town today?

Learning to spell can be a challenge but if you work at it, you will get better and better.
After you have finished each unit in this book, think about what you have learnt.
If anything is still a little confusing, ask your teacher for help.
And remember, you will learn to spell unknown or tricky words faster if you practise spelling these words every day.

**LOOK, COVER, WRITE, CHECK**

**Practise your weekly Spelling List this way:**

1. **LOOK carefully at the word.**
2. **COVER the word.**
3. **WRITE the word from memory.**
4. **CHECK to see if your spelling is correct.**

# CONTENTS ›

## Term 3

| | Topic | Focus | Spelling Words | Word Knowledge |
|---|---|---|---|---|
| 21 | Vowel digraphs | 'ow' sound as in sound, cow | inside, it's, tree, cake, best, sound, count, loud, allow, prowl | Pronouns |
| 22 | Vowel digraphs | 'oy' sound as in boy, coin | fell, long, movie, soccer, how, choice, annoy, join, cowboy, spoil | Sentences |
| 23 | Vowel digraphs | 'air' sound as in chair, bare | also, know, last, sleep, swimming, air, chair, bare, square, dairy | Conjunctions |
| 24 | Vowel digraphs | 'ar' sound as in path, car, half | around, don't, just, told, yes, calm, palm, tomato, banana, bath | Prepositions |
| 25 | Revision | | | |
| 26 | Letter combinations | 'u' sound as in mug, come | today, beach, killed, finished, funny, done, undone, welcome, someone, anyone | Question marks |
| 27 | Letter combinations | 'e' sound as in let, bread | book, here, things, yesterday, computer, headache, weather, spread, head, pencil | Exclamation marks |
| 28 | Letter combinations | 'o' sound as in hot, was | help, zoo, now, ride, castle, hospital, knock, knot, wash, what | Statements |
| 29 | Letter combinations | 'i' sound as in bit, gym | toy, cousins, look, more, tried, quiz, chill, gym, Egypt, prison | Speech marks |
| 30 | Revision | | | |

## Term 4

| | Topic | Focus | Spelling Words | Word Knowledge |
|---|---|---|---|---|
| 31 | Consonant sounds | 'c' sound as in clown, king, back | find, four, I'm, happily, started, castle, calm, comb, rocket, kettle | Speech marks |
| 32 | Consonant sounds | 'j' sound as in jug, giraffe | dragon, much, rabbit, five, turned, giraffe, jelly, cabbage, magic, jetty | Plurals |
| 33 | Consonant sounds | 's' sound as in sun, circle | another, make cousins, breakfast, chips, circus, somebody, seventy, parcel, bicycle | Compound verbs |
| 34 | Consonant sounds | 'z' sound as in zoo, says, present | couldn't, present, together, walk, great, zone, quiz, nose, busy, papers | Compound nouns |
| 35 | Revision | | | |
| 36 | 'i' (igh) sound | 'i' sound as in high, light | loved, magic, work, coming, someone, right, frightened, highway, lighting, high | Past, present and future tense verbs |
| 37 | 'er' sound | 'er' sound as in her, third, fur, early, worm | team, thing, always, boat, door, furniture, nurse, person, birth, first | Noun suffixes |
| 38 | 'w' sound | 'w' sound as in water, what | teacher, its, princess, shopping, until, whisper, where, worm, wife, when | Alliteration |
| 39 | 'qu' sound | 'qu' sound as in queen, squeal | pool, take, well, animals, horse, quick, quarter, square, squeeze, quit | Onomatopoeia |
| 40 | Revision | | | |

# To the Teacher ›

## About the **Essential Spelling Skills** series

The **Essential Spelling Skills** series is a sequential, developmental spelling program that will provide primary students in Grades 3 to 8 with strategies and skills to become independent spellers in English. Each book has been designed as a full year's spelling program consisting of 40 three-page units of work.

## Learning to spell strategies

Good spellers use these strategies to help them become successful:

- **Phonological strategies** – how word and letter combinations sound.
- **Visual strategies** – how word and letter combinations look.
- **Morphemic strategies** – how words take different spellings when they change form (for example, church – churches).
- **Etymological strategies** – how words are spelt and where they come from (for example, aeroplane = 'aero' meaning air + 'plane' meaning a flat surface).
- **Inquiry strategies** – how to use learning tools such as a dictionary or thesaurus to spell difficult or unknown words.

These strategies are the basis for learning to spell at every level of this series. In the early levels – Grades 3, 4, and 5 – the emphasis is on visual and phonological strategies to allow children to develop a firm base on which to build more complex understandings of English spelling. In the upper levels – Grades 6, 7 and 8 – there is an increasing emphasis on developing morphemic knowledge and understanding English constructions.

A useful strategy to assist the students' learning, as well as provide the teacher with valuable guidance to students' progress, is the 'Have-A-Go-Card'. To make the simplest 'Have-A-Go-Card', divide a sheet of card or paper into three columns. The students have a go at spelling the word in the first two columns. They tick the spelling they think is correct and check this spelling with their teacher. The teacher confirms the correct spelling and writes it in the third column.

| | | |
|---|---|---|
| beter ✓ | better | better |
| were | where ✓ | where |
| brake ✓ | break | break |
| realy | really ✓ | really |
| wobling | wobbling ✓ | wobbling |

## How to use the **Essential Spelling Skills** series

This spelling program consists of 40 units of work – ten units per term. Each unit consists of three pages of work including sufficient activities for a five-day spelling program. The first two pages in each unit concentrate on developing spelling strategies to tackle unknown words and the third page allows students to learn more about English, including grammar and writing skills. The units include written activities that are designed to show that spelling is not an isolated skill, but is essential for the development of literacy skills. An assessment program is built into each unit and is usually completed on the fifth day. This is designed to help the teacher test students' spelling knowledge on a regular basis.

## **Example unit** – Term 3 Week 1

The following example shows how a unit of work can be broken down into a week's program using the five spelling strategies. It demonstrates how each unit contains one full week's work relating specifically to spelling, but also incorporates reading and writing.

| Unit 21 | Focus | Spelling strategy | Teacher preparation | Activities/tasks |
|---|---|---|---|---|
| **Day 1** | 'ow' sound as in sound, cow | Phonological | Make a chart with the Word List or write the Word List on the board. These words need to be displayed for the whole week as this is the unit focus. | **1.** As a class, read all the words on the Word List. Note that the same sound can be made by using two different letter patterns, for example: '**ou**' as in found, sound, count and '**ow**' as in now, how, cow.<br>**2.** Choose words from the list and ask students to use them (orally) in a complete sentence.<br>**3.** Talk about activity 1 (orally) before students complete it in the student book.<br>**4.** Students complete activities 2 to 4 to consolidate learning relating to the '**ow**' sound. |
| **Day 2** | | Phonological | Copy the rhyme on a chart or on the board, making it large enough for students to read. | **1.** Reinforce point 1 from Day 1 above.<br>**2.** Talk about activities 5 to 7 (orally) before you ask students to complete them.<br>**3.** Complete the **Rhyme Time** activity to consolidate learning relating to the '**ow**' sound. |
| **Day 3** | | Common words (there are ten spelling words – five common words and five 'ou' sound words) | Copy the ten spelling words on the board.<br>Students learn these words by applying the strategy:<br>**Look** – at the word<br>**Cover** – the word<br>**Write** – the word<br>**Check** – the spelling | **1.** As a class, read the spelling words. Choose students to use these words (orally) in complete sentences.<br>**2.** Play games with the spelling words to help the students memorise them. For example, ask students to close their eyes and attempt to spell a given word, or play snap and memory games with the words on cards.<br>**3.** Students copy the spelling words in their book.<br>**4.** During the week, students need to practise spelling these words. Tell students that these words will be tested at the end of the week. |
| **Day 4** | | Word knowledge (inquiry strategy) | Copy the definition of a pronoun on the board and leave it for the rest of the week:<br>*A **pronoun** is a word that is used in place of a noun, for example: he, she, it.* | **1.** Reinforce the purpose of a pronoun.<br>**2.** As a class, practise substituting pronouns for nouns in selected sentences.<br>**3.** Students complete the activities in their books. |
| **Day 5** | Assessment | Visual and phonological | | **1.** Reinforce concepts and skills taught during the week.<br>**2.** Dictate the ten spelling words to students.<br>**3.** Record any relevant assessment information, for example, common errors made by students. (Test)<br>**4.** After finishing the spelling test, students complete the Writing activity to extend their word knowledge and comprehension skills. |

# Unit 1

## FOCUS > 'sh' sound

**RULE**

The '**sh**' sound can be used at the beginning, middle or end of a word.
For example: **sh**ut (at the beginning), cru**sh**es (in the middle), ca**sh** (at the end).

**1** Choose a word from the Word List for each picture.
Write the words in alphabetical order in your book.

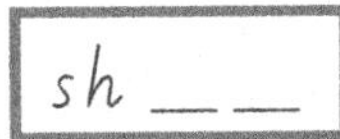
sh _ _

_ _ _ sh

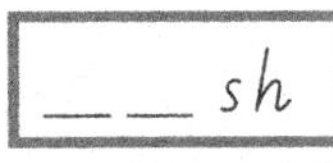
_ _ sh

_ _ sh

sh _ _ _

_ _ _ sh

sh _ _ _

sh _ _ _

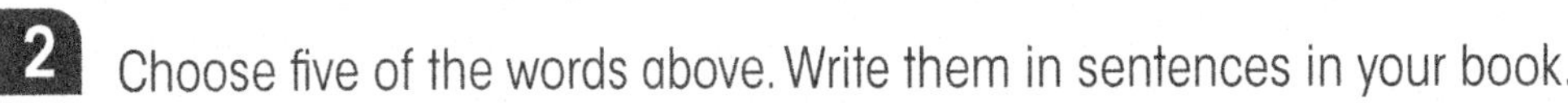

**2** Choose five of the words above. Write them in sentences in your book.

**3** Find words from the Word List that have a similar meaning to these words.
Write the words in sentences in your book. The first one has been done for you.

to run very fast → *dash* *I must dash home to get my book.*

to long for or hope for something →

to call out loud →

the sun does this →

you find this on the seashore →

these animals have woolly coats →

they swim in the sea →

**4** Change one letter in each word to make a new word.
Write the new words in your book. The first one has been done for you.

a.

| s | h | o | n | e |
|---|---|---|---|---|
| *s* | *h* | *i* | *n* | *e* |

b.

| s | h | e | e | t |
|---|---|---|---|---|
| | | | | |

c.

| s | h | o | p |
|---|---|---|---|
| | | | |

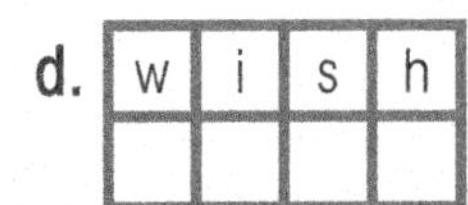

d.

| w | i | s | h |
|---|---|---|---|
| | | | |

e.

| m | a | s | h |
|---|---|---|---|
| | | | |

**Word LIST**

ship
sheep
shell
fish
brush
crash
wish
fishes
cash
wash
shout
shirt
shine
shin
mushroom
she
shut
wishes
flashes
crushes
shift
shelf
shock
dash
dish
ash
dishwasher
shade
sharp
sheet
flashing
wishful
seashore
dishes

**5** Write as many words as you can in your book, using the magic word machines. Write the words in your book under the correct heading:

a. 'sh–' at the beginning

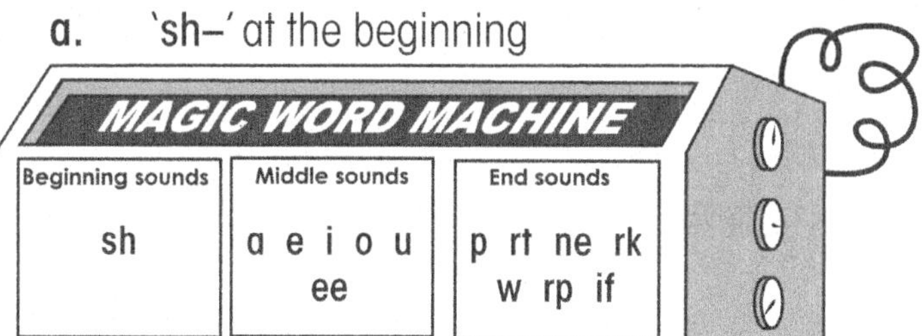


b. 'sh' in the middle

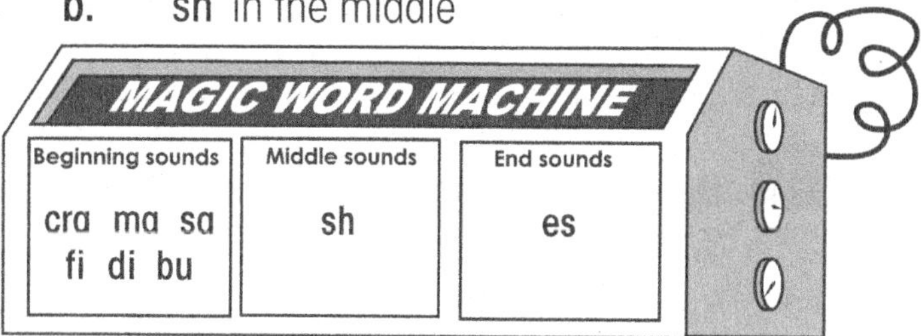


c. '–sh' at the end

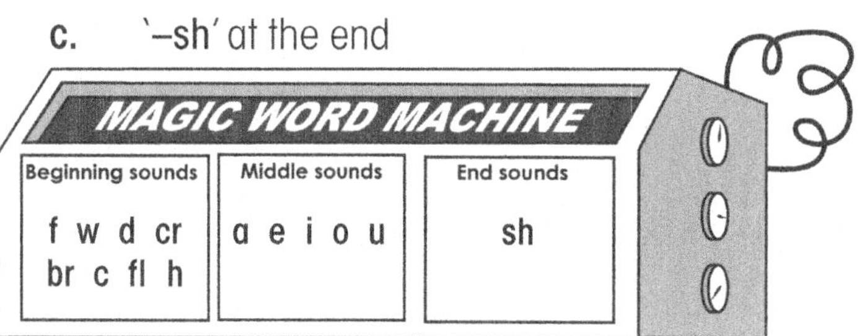


**6** Choose the correct word. Write the words in complete sentences in your book.

a. The car lights were (flashing / dashing) in the dark.
b. Please (shut / shift) the door when you go out.
c. We use a (brush / bash) to comb our hair.
d. When Simon touched the electric fence he got a (shine / shock).
e. Lila will (wash / wish) before she leaves.
f. Jonah found a (sharp / shell) on the seashore.

**7** Find words from the Word List in this word search puzzle. Write them in your book.

| | | | | | | | |
|---|---|---|---|---|---|---|---|
| v | z | s | h | a | r | p | d |
| w | a | s | h | o | y | r | i |
| s | s | h | o | u | t | s | s |
| s | h | i | r | t | x | h | h |
| m | u | s | h | r | o | o | m |
| q | k | p | b | r | u | s | h |

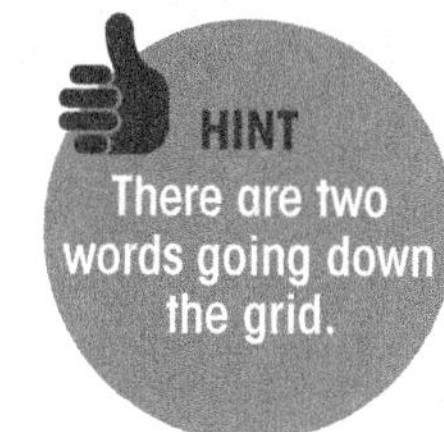


**RHYME time** › Copy this rhyme into your book and then ...

1. Circle the words that end in '**–ash**' or '**–ashes**'.
2. Draw a square around the word that ends in '**–osh**'.
3. Underline the word that ends in '**–ishes**'.
4. Write more words that end in '**–ash**' and '**–ish**' in your book.

*Come over and splash in the water!*
*It's great to splosh in the wet,*
*Watch out for the splashes and splishes,*
*How much wetter can anyone get?*

# WORD KNOWLEDGE › Compound words

**RULE**

**Compound words** are made when two words are joined to make one bigger word.
For example: *sea* + *shore* = *seashore*, *wish* + *bone* = *wishbone*.

**1** Draw a line to show the two small words in each compound word, for example: ear / ring.
Write the words in sentences in your book.

cupboard toothbrush birthday dishwasher earring

**2** Find compound words beginning with the word 'sun'.
Write the compound words in your book.

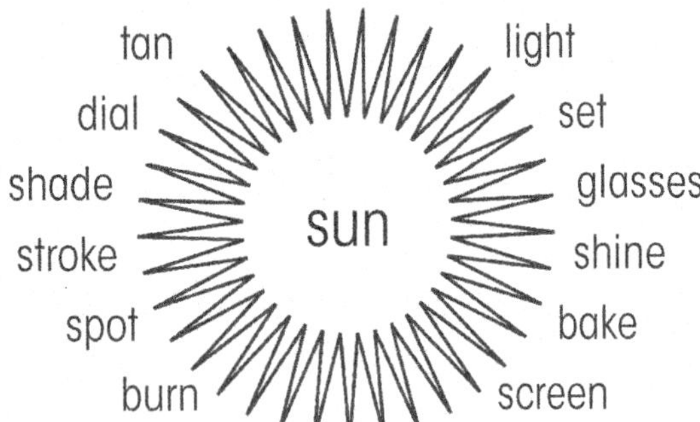


*sun + shine = sunshine*

______________________

______________________

______________________

______________________

______________________

______________________

## COMMON WORDS ›

**1** Choose words from the Spelling List to fill the gaps.
Write the complete sentences in your book.

a. Tom's grandpa _ _ _ _ him to the sing sing.
b. The _ _ _ _ _ day, I went to visit my aunty.
c. My teacher said it is _ _ _ _ to be polite.
d. The time is _ _ _ _ _ three thirty.
e. It is Leti's birthday _ _ _ _ _ tomorrow.

Weekly Spelling List to be tested at the end of the week

**Spelling LIST**

party
about
took
good
other
shut
fish
crashes
shout
dishes

**2** Write the words from the Spelling List with 'sh' in them in sentences in your book.

**LOOK, COVER, WRITE, CHECK**

Practise your weekly spelling this way:
1. LOOK carefully at the word.
2. COVER the word.
3. WRITE the word from memory.
4. CHECK to see if your spelling is correct.

**Writing activity › Lost in the Bush**

- What would you do if you were lost in the bush? What are the dangers? How would you survive? Write about being lost in the bush and what you would do to survive.

# FOCUS > 'th' sound

**RULE**

The '**th**' sound can be used at the beginning, middle or end of a word.
For example: **th**ud (at the beginning), bro**th**er (in the middle), pa**th** (at the end).

**Word LIST**

| | |
|---|---|
| bath | father |
| thin | bother |
| third | thong |
| thumb | youth |
| moth | thorn |
| north | thunder |
| south | three |
| birthday | thirty |
| mouth | third |
| mouthful | sixth |
| tooth | thistle |
| teeth | thirsty |
| brother | froth |
| mother | thousand |
| thick | thug |
| thank | thought |
| think | with |
| thin | both |

**1** Choose a word from the Word List for each picture.
Write the words in alphabetical order in your book.

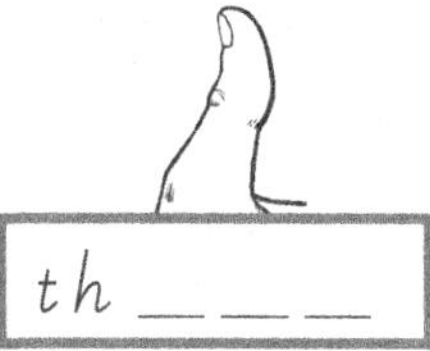
th _ _ _

_ _ th

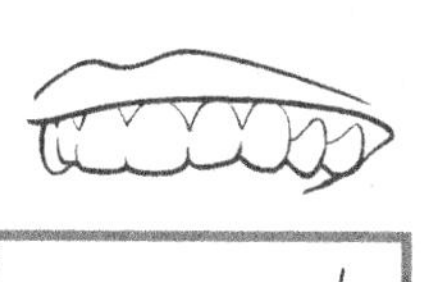
_ _ _ th

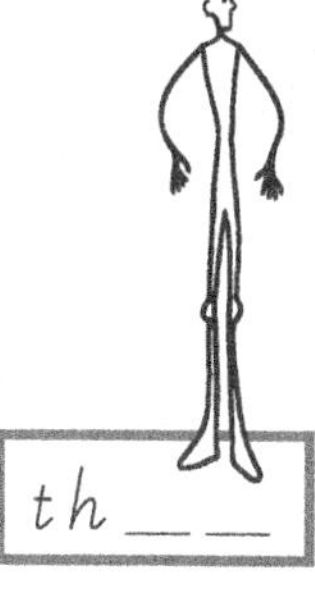
th _ _

_ _ _ th

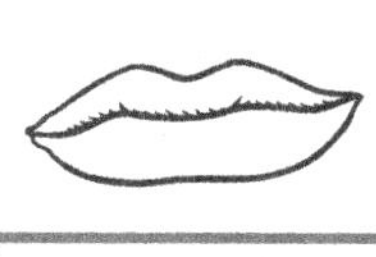
_ _ _ th

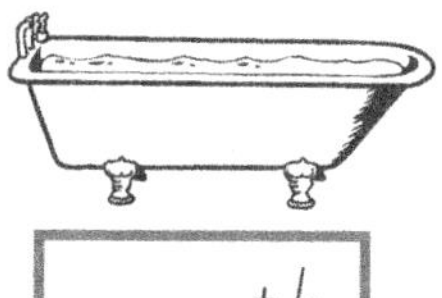
_ _ th

_ _ _ th _ _ _

**2** Choose five of the words above. Write them in sentences in your book.

**3** Find words from the Word List that have a similar meaning to these words.
Write the words in sentences in your book. The first one has been done for you.

the number after 'second' → *third* *Lila came third in the race.*

the opposite of thick → ______

you use these for chewing → ______

ten plus ten plus ten equals this → ______

your female parent → ______

a prickly weed → ______

the opposite of north → ______

this celebrates the day that you were born → ______

**4** Change one letter in each word to make a new word.
Write the new words in your book. The first one has been done for you.

**a.**

| t | h | u | d |
|---|---|---|---|
| *t* | *h* | *u* | *g* |

**b.**

| t | h | a | n | k |
|---|---|---|---|---|
| | | | | |

**c.**

| f | o | r | t | h |
|---|---|---|---|---|
| | | | | |

**d.**

| b | a | t | h |
|---|---|---|---|
| | | | |

**e.**

| b | o | t | h |
|---|---|---|---|
| | | | |

**f.**

| t | h | u | m | p |
|---|---|---|---|---|
| | | | | |

**5** Write as many words as you can in your book, using the magic word machines. Write the words in your book under the correct heading:

a. 'th–' at the beginning

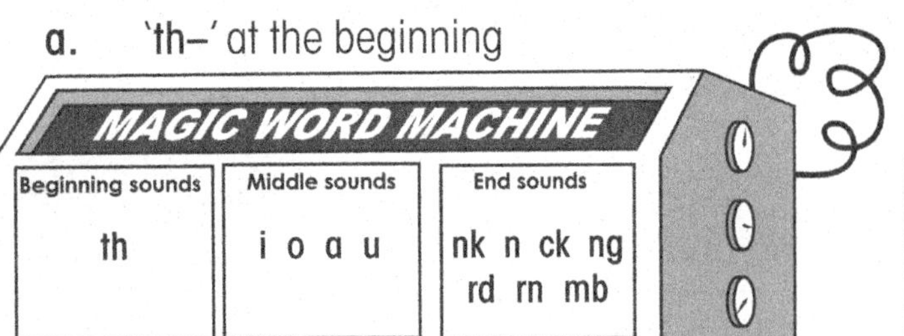


b. 'th' in the middle

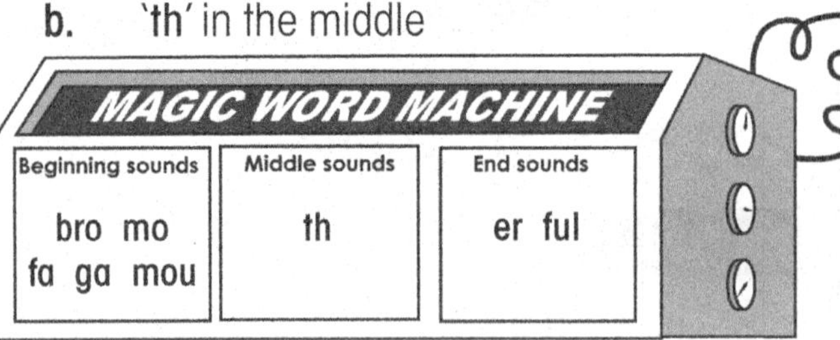


c. '–th' at the end

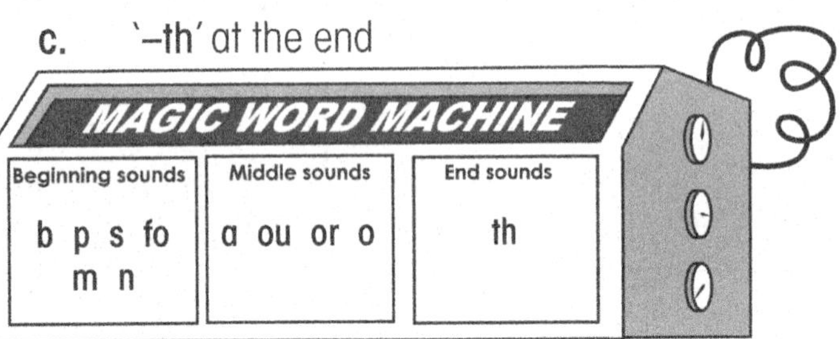


**6** Choose the correct word. Write the words in complete sentences in your book.

a. Mrs Bula broke a (tooth / teeth) when she chewed on the bone.
b. When we saw the ice-cream cone, we (bath / both) wanted it.
c. The (mouth / moth) fluttered towards the light.
d. Jenifa wanted to (thank / thick) her aunty for the gift.
e. My father is (thirty / third) years old.
f. Rina broke her (thumb / thing) when she fell over.
g. It is too much (bother / brother) to walk to the market today.

**7** Find words from the Word List in this word search puzzle. Write them in your book.

| b | a | t | h | z | b | y | c |
|---|---|---|---|---|---|---|---|
| w | c | t | h | i | c | k | v |
| b | i | r | t | h | d | a | y |
| t | h | i | r | s | t | y | x |
| q | t | h | a | n | k | r | f |
| g | t | o | o | t | h | t | y |

**RHYME time** › Copy this rhyme into your book and then ...

1. Circle all the words that begin with '**th–**'.
2. Draw a square around the word that ends with '**–th**'.
3. Underline the word with '**th**' in the middle.
4. Make up a different ending for the rhyme and write it in your book.

***Thirsty Tim***
*I had a little brother,*
*His name was Thirsty Tim.*
*I put him in the bath tub*
*To see if he could swim.*
*He drank up all the water,*
*He ate up all the soap.*
*He died last night.*
*With a bubble in his throat.*

# WORD KNOWLEDGE › Upper case letters

**RULE**

**Proper nouns** are the names of people, places, days and months.
We use upper case letters at the beginning of proper nouns.
For example: *Tom* (person), *Madang* (play), *Monday* (day), *February* (month).

**1** Write the months of the year in order in your book. Check your spelling with a friend. Don't forget to use upper case letters.

**2** Write the days of the week in order in your book. Check your spelling with a friend. Don't forget to use upper case letters.

**3** Copy this envelope into your book. Write your full address on it, including:

a. your first and last name
b. your house number and/or the name of your street
c. the name of your town or village
d. the name of your country

**HINT**
Don't forget to use upper case letters for the beginning of names and places.

# COMMON WORDS ›

**1** Choose words from the Spelling List to fill the gaps. Write the complete sentences in your book.

a. There were fifty _ _ _ _ _ _ at the market today.
b. The teacher said, "Please _ _ _ the book back on the table."
c. Kela is my best _ _ _ _ _ _.
d. The boy said that he _ _ _ _ _ _ take the money.
e. Josepha and Colitha took _ _ _ _ _ shoes off.

**2** Write the words from the Spelling List with '**th**' in them in sentences in your book.

Weekly Spelling List to be tested at the end of the week

**Spelling LIST**

- people
- didn't
- friend
- their
- put
- thick
- thin
- bath
- mother
- birthday

**Writing activity › Write a Letter**

- Write a letter to a friend or relation. Address the envelope correctly. Use upper case letters for the names of people and places.

# Unit 3

## FOCUS › 'f' sound

**RULE**

The 'f' sound can be made with the letter '**f**', the letters '**ff**' or the letters '**ph**'. For example: **f**un, chie**f** (the letter '**f**'), co**ff**ee, sni**ff** (the letters '**ff**'), **ph**oto, gra**ph** (the letters '**ph**').

**1** Choose a word from the Word List for each picture. Write the words in alphabetical order in your book.

f _ _ _

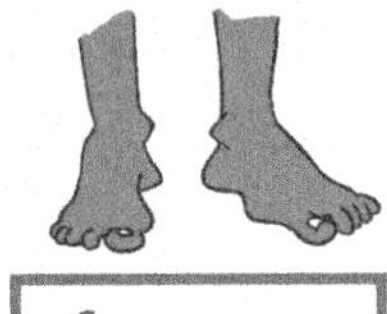
f _ _ _

_ _ _ ph _ _ _

_ _ _ _ _ ff _

f _ _ _

f _ _ _ _ _ _ _

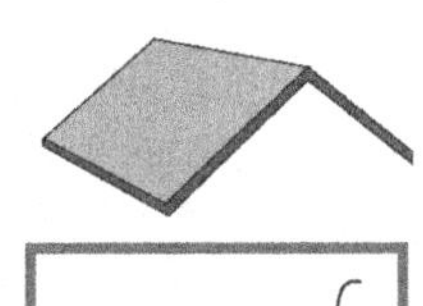
_ _ _ f

ph _ _ _

**2** Choose five of the words above. Write them in sentences in your book.

**3** Copy these words into your book. Circle the odd one out.

| | | | | | |
|---|---|---|---|---|---|
| **a.** | fun | first | face | six | four |
| **b.** | off | biff | grunt | huff | puff |
| **c.** | phone | phoning | next | telephone | phoned |
| **d.** | four | five | coffee | fourteen | fifteen |
| **e.** | different | stiff | sniff | photo | gruff |

**4** Find words from the Word List that have a similar meaning to these words. Write the words in sentences in your book. The first one has been done for you.

a picture taken with a camera → *photo* *I took a photo with my new camera.*

very big, overweight →

a baby horse →

what you do when you run out of breath →

a short word for telephone →

an animal with huge ears and a trunk →

**Word LIST**

fish
feet
foal
phone
photo
elephant
roof
coffee
giraffe
football
fire
Friday
first
fun
sniff
huff
puff
gruff
roof
off
flag
fat
full
nephew
graph
face
surf
fall
four
fire
surf
turf
friend

**5** Find rhyming words for these words from the Word List.
Write each pair of rhyming words in your book.

toffee ball huff your race goal thirst tire turf stiff meet bone

**6** Read the words in the Word List aloud. Say what letter or letters make the '**f**' sound.

**7** Make '**ff**' words by joining the letters in the circles. The first one has been done for you.

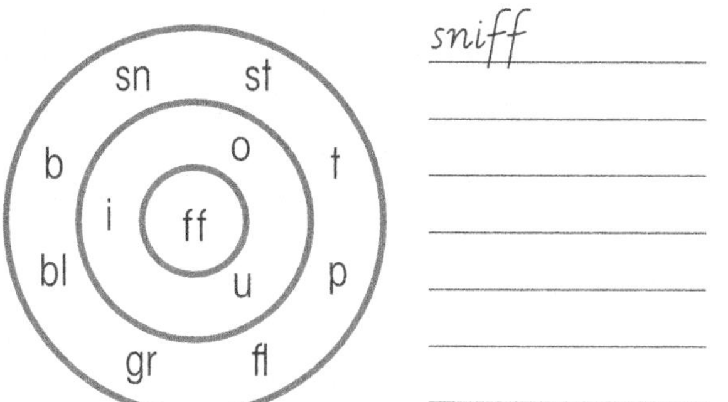


**8** Make '**f**' words by connecting the letters in the boxes. The first one has been done for you.

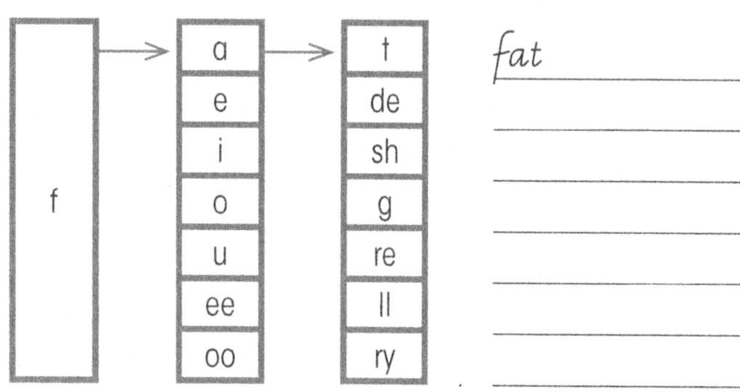


**9** Choose words from the Word List to fill the gaps.
Write the complete sentences in your book.

**a.** We have our spelling test on _ _ _ _ _ _ _ _.

**b.** My dad likes a cup of _ _ _ _ _ _ in the morning.

**c.** The wolf said, "I'll _ _ _ _ and I'll _ _ _ _ and I'll blow your house down."

**d.** The _ _ _ _ _ _ _ has a very long neck.

**e.** I saw the dog _ _ _ _ _ the sausages on the table.

**f.** If you eat too much unhealthy food, you will get very _ _ _.

**RHYME time** › Copy this rhyme into your book and then ...

1. What is the name of the nephew?
2. What is the name of the nephew's aunt?
3. What is a shorter name for Freddy?
4. Write three '**ph–**' words and two words beginning with a capital '**F**' in your book.

*"Phone your nephew Freddy, Freda.*
*Phone your nephew Fred."*
*"No! I'm always phoning Freddy*
*So let Fred phone me instead!"*

# WORD KNOWLEDGE › Homophones

**RULE**

A **homophone** is a word with the same sound as another word, but with different spelling and a different meaning, for example: *see* and *sea*.

**1** Choose homophones from the Word Bank to match these words.

**Word BANK**

pan see to nose sum flour cheap not
meet flower sea two knot knows some

| | | | | | | | |
|---|---|---|---|---|---|---|---|
| a. | see _______ | b. | to _______ | c. | nose _______ | d. | sum _______ |
| e. | flour _______ | f. | cheep _______ | g. | not _______ | h. | meet _______ |

**2** Copy these sentences into your book. Circle the two homophones in each sentence.

a. Mum might meet the butcher when she buys the meat.
b. Even though the sky was blue, the wind blew strongly.
c. After the thief was caught, he had to go to face the judge in court.
d. Is it right to write my name in the book?

# COMMON WORDS ›

**1** Choose words from the Spelling List to fill the gaps.
Write the complete sentences in your book.

a. Jenifa jumped _ _ _ _ the log that was lying on the track.
b. When Simon got his new glasses he could _ _ _ much better.
c. Letti showed _ _ where the treasure was.
d. When my aunty was a _ _ _ _ she was very small.
e. The teacher asked, "Which _ _ _ or _ _ _ _ stole the chocolates?"

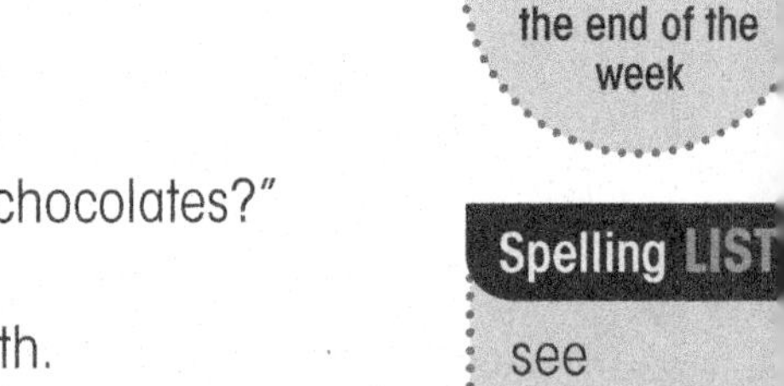


**Spelling LIST**

see
girl
boy
over
us
face
roof
fifth
phone
stiff

**2** Write these numbers in full in your book: 4th, 5th, 6th, 7th, 8th, 9th.

**Writing activity › How Does a Telephone Work?**

- Draw some pictures and write some labels to show how a telephone works.

# Unit 4

## FOCUS > 'ch' sound

**RULE**

The '**ch**' sound can be used at the beginning, middle or end of a word.
For example: **ch**op (at the beginning), tea**ch**er (in the middle), ea**ch** (at the end).
It can also be used with the letter '**t**', for example: 'ca**tch**'.

**Word LIST**

| | |
|---|---|
| chips | catch |
| chick | fetch |
| chop | peach |
| teacher | beaches |
| lunch | each |
| beach | scratch |
| children | pitch |
| hatch | patch |
| itch | blotch |
| witch | child |
| pinch | stitch |
| chain | clutch |
| preacher | chat |
| cheek | cheap |
| branch | peaches |
| bunch | twitch |
| crunch | cheep |
| crutch | crutch |
| match | mulch |
| sketch | pinch |

**1** Choose a word from the Word List for each picture. Write the words in alphabetical order in your book.

ch _ _ _

ch _ _ _

_ _ _ ch

_ _ tch

ch _ _ _ _ _ _

_ _ _ ch

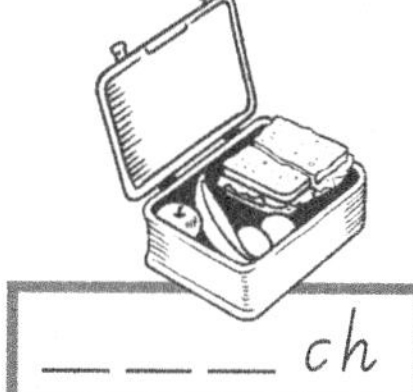

_ _ _ ch

_ _ tch

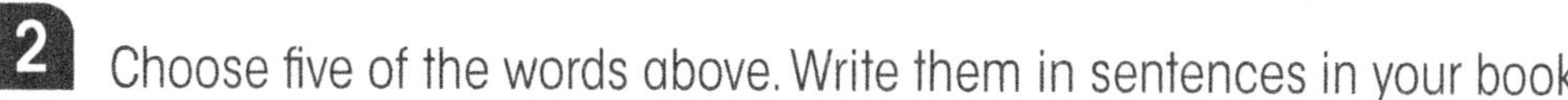

**2** Choose five of the words above. Write them in sentences in your book.

**3** Copy these words into your book. Circle the odd one out.

| | | | | | |
|---|---|---|---|---|---|
| **a.** | lunch | bunch | hunch | dinner | munch |
| **b.** | itch | witch | stitch | pitch | blotch |
| **c.** | chip | chop | slip | chat | china |
| **d.** | children | child | chain | chat | clip |
| **e.** | chick | cats | chicken | chicks | chicory |

**4** Find words from the Word List that have a similar meaning to these words. Write the words in sentences in your book. The first one has been done for you.

you want to scratch this → *itch* *I had an itch on my leg*

a round soft juicy fruit →

the side of your face below your eye →

a part that sticks out from the trunk of a tree →

a row of metal rings connected to each other →

to make a quick drawing of something →

## 5

Change one letter in each word to make a new word.
Write the new words in your book. The first one has been done for you.

a. match — *patch*
b. switch
c. cheep
d. clutch
e. hitch
f. munch

## 6

Write two sentences for each of these words in your book to show two different meanings for each word.

chop match chip watch

## 7

Choose the correct word. Write the words in complete sentences in your book.

a. There are fifty-one (child / children) at our school.
b. When the branch fell down it (scratched / hatched) the car.
c. When Letti broke her leg she needed (hutches / crutches).
d. The doctor said, "I will have to (switch / stitch) that cut."
e. The tree had a nice new (bunch / branch) of bananas.
f. Dad was towing the car with a (chin / chain) but it broke.

## 8

Copy this crossword in your book. Write the correct word for each clue and find the mystery word. Write the mystery word in a sentence in your book.

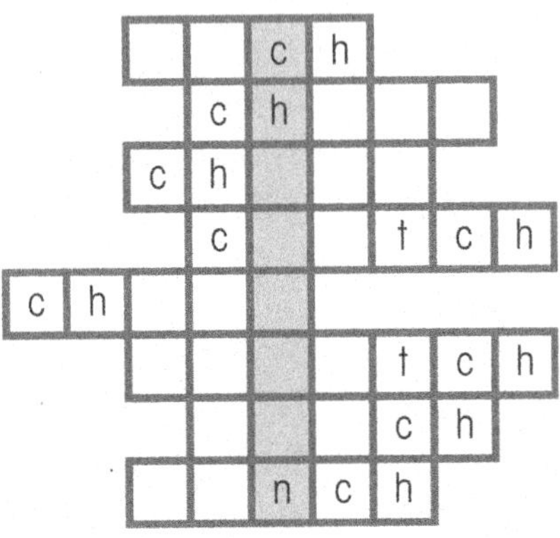


... if you have one of these, you want to scratch it
... small pieces of fried potato, served with fish
... a baby chicken
... to grab hold of something tightly
... a small person
... if you have an itch, you want to do this to it
... the sandy part of the land near the sea
... what you eat in the middle of the day

### RHYME time › Copy this rhyme into your book and then ...

1. Circle all the words that end in '**–itch**'.
2. Draw a square around the word that ends in '**–ich**'.
3. Write two sentences to show the different meanings for '**which**' and '**witch**'.

*Which witch is which?*
*One witch had an itch,*
*Another witch had a twitch.*
*So one witch started to twitch,*
*And the other witch started to itch.*
*Now it's hard to tell . . .*
*Which witch is which.*

# WORD KNOWLEDGE > Abbreviations

**RULE**

An **abbreviation** is a shortened word.
For example, the shortened word for *television* is *tv*, the shortened word for *doctor* is *Dr*, the shortened word for *Mister* is *Mr* and the shortened word for *Tuesday* is *Tues*.

**1** Copy this table into your book.
Write the abbreviations for the days of the week.

| Monday | Tuesday | Wednesday | Thursday | Friday | Saturday | Sunday |
|---|---|---|---|---|---|---|
| | | | | | | |

**2** Use the Abbreviation Box to find the correct abbreviation for each of these words.
Write each pair of words in your book.

photograph refrigerator football telephone advertisement January

**Abbreviation BOX**

phone
ad
footy
fridge
photo
Jan

## COMMON WORDS >

**1** Choose words from the Spelling List to fill the gaps.
Write the complete sentences in your book.

a. It is _ _ _ _ turn to go first today.
b. Lela jumped _ _ _ the horse.
c. I like chops for _ _ _ _ _ _.
d. This is the story of _ _ _ _ _ little pigs.
e. My dad _ _ _ _ _ to have a sleep in the afternoon.

**2** Add '**–ed**' to these words from the Spelling List.
Write them in sentences in your book.

pitch match

**Spelling LIST**

your
off
three
dinner
likes
lunch
match
child
pitch
beach

**Writing activity > A Fight with a Friend**

- Have you ever had a fight with your friend? Write about what happened. Describe how you made up. Make a list of ways to be friendly with people, rather than fight with them.

# FOCUS > 'sh' 'th' 'f' 'ch' sounds

**1** Copy these tables into your book. Fill the gaps with the words to match the letter patterns.

| 'sh' words | |
|---|---|
| ship | cash |
| shop | wish |
| ______ | ______ |
| ______ | ______ |
| ______ | ______ |

| 'th' words | |
|---|---|
| thick | with |
| thin | path |
| ______ | ______ |
| ______ | ______ |
| ______ | ______ |

| 'ch' words | |
|---|---|
| chip | peach |
| chop | each |
| ______ | ______ |
| ______ | ______ |
| ______ | ______ |

**2** Write these words beginning with '**ch–**' in sentences in your book.

cheek chop cheep cheap

**3** Choose the correct word. Write the words in complete sentences in your book.

a. Jim was very (thirty / thirsty) after running the race.
b. Dad tried to (catch / scratch) the foal, but it ran away.
c. The (dishwasher / shelf) was full of dirty (dishes / fishes).
d. "Please take my (photo / face)!" said Leila.
e. If you have an (eye / itch) you have to (scratch / sniff) it.
f. Billy had a (tooth / teeth)ache.

**4** Copy this word grid in your book. Use the clues to find words.
Write the words in your book. The first one has been done for you.

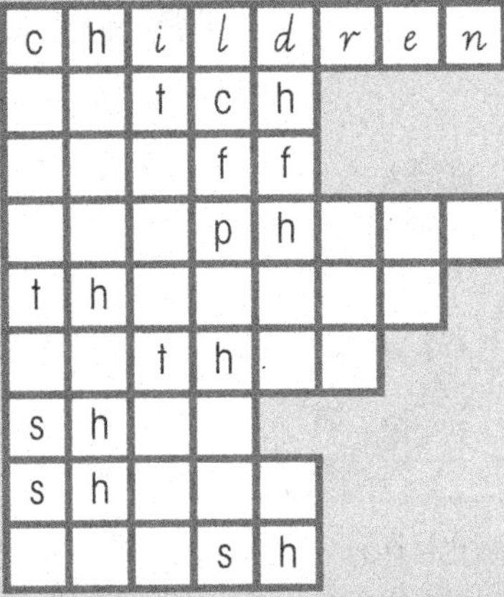


... more than one child → *children*
... a woman with magic powers
... you use your nose to do this
... a very large animal
... a loud noise that comes with lightning
... your male parent
... to close something
... to call out very loudly
... to squeeze between your fingers

**5** Find small '**sh**' or '**ch**' words inside these larger words. The first one has been done for you.

| | | | |
|---|---|---|---|
| brush → *rush* | crash → ______ | peach → ______ | flashes → ______ |
| children → ______ | chickens → ______ | wash → ______ | wishful → ______ |

**6** Use the picture clues to complete the words in the frames. Write the words in your book.

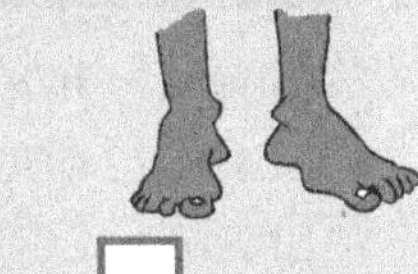
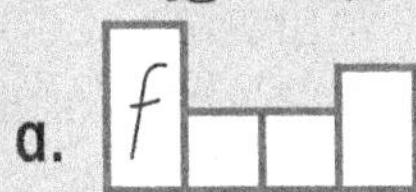

a. *f* _ _ _
b. _ _ _ _ *f f* _ _
c. *f* _ _ _ _
d. *p h* _ _ _ _
e. *f* _ _ _
f. _ _ _ *f*

**7** Copy these words into your book. Circle the odd one out.

| | | | | | |
|---|---|---|---|---|---|
| a. | branch | bunch | lunch | chop | munch |
| b. | catch | hatch | match | pitch | patch |
| c. | huff | sniff | surf | puff | gruff |
| d. | coffee | toffee | fish | giraffe | |
| e. | photo | telephone | television | photograph | phone |
| f. | wishes | flashes | dishes | shut | crashes |

**8** Change one letter to make a new word that matches the clue.
Write the new words in your book. The first one has been done for you.

a. wish (to clean something by washing it in water) → *wash*
b. think (the opposite of thin)
c. thing (a rubber shoe)
d. dish (it has fins and swims in the sea)
e. turf (big white waves)
f. match (chickens do this when they are born)
g. beach (a soft fruit with a big stone inside it)

**9** Find the '**sh**', '**th**', '**ch**', '**tch**', '**ph**', '**f**' and '**ff**' words in this word search puzzle.
Write the words in alphabetical order in your book.

| | | | | | | | | |
|---|---|---|---|---|---|---|---|---|
| t | h | a | n | k | w | i | s | h |
| z | y | t | e | n | t | h | h | q |
| m | t | h | i | r | s | t | y | s |
| c | h | i | l | d | r | e | n | h |
| h | v | n | p | h | o | t | o | l |
| o | c | h | i | c | k | s | m | f |
| p | e | l | e | p | h | a | n | t |
| a | s | h | n | e | p | h | e | w |
| c | a | t | c | h | t | h | i | n |

**! Challenge**

- Copy this tongue twister into your book. Try and say it quickly three times out loud.
- Write a '**sh**' or '**th**' tongue twister of your own.

**She sells seashells by the seashore.**

# FOCUS > Long vowel a–e

**RULE**

Remember, **long vowels** 'say' their name, for example: **a** – gr**a**de.
The '**e**' at the end of the word makes the vowel say its own name.

**Word LIST**

| | |
|---|---|
| face | frame |
| place | ape |
| grade | cape |
| made | grape |
| cage | late |
| page | save |
| bake | race |
| cake | space |
| same | blade |
| game | grace |
| shape | fade |
| scrape | spade |
| pace | stage |
| blade | wage |
| rage | sale |
| lake | scale |
| wake | tale |
| whale | came |
| gave | tame |
| flame | tape |
| mate | cave |
| shade | stale |
| shame | grave |
| shave | behav |

**1** Copy this table into your book. Fill the gaps with '**a–e**' words to match the letter patterns. The first one has been done for you.

| –ale | –ace | –age | –ade | –ame | –ape |
|---|---|---|---|---|---|
| *sale*<br>*scale*<br>*stale*<br>*tale*<br>*whale* | | | | | |

**2** Write one word from each section of the table above in a sentence in your book.

**3** Choose words from the Word List to fill the gaps.
Write the complete sentences in your book.

a. The farmer used his s_ _ _ _ to dig the hard soil.
b. The smallest girl in class won the 100 metres r_ _ _.
c. I saw a big a_ _ swinging through the trees.
d. The f_ _ _ _s from the fire died down.
e. I had to s_ _ _ _ _ the mud from my shoes.
f. The rocket shot up into s_ _ _ _.

**4** Write as many words as you can in your book, using the magic word machines.

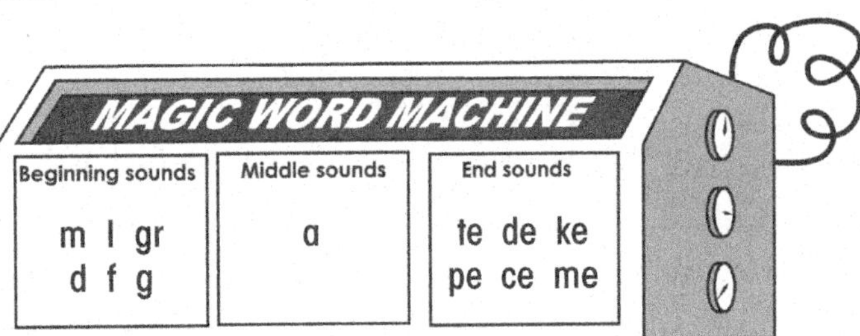


MAGIC WORD MACHINE

| Beginning sounds | Middle sounds | End sounds |
|---|---|---|
| c g s<br>w sh | a | ve de me<br>d t |

**5** Write these words from the Word List in your book in alphabetical order.

shade spade stage sale scale stale shape scrape save shave

**6** Choose the correct word. Write the words in complete sentences in your book.

a. Anis (make / made) a new cover for the seat.
b. Please shut the (gate / cave) after you go in.
c. Our team won the (came / game) in the last ten minutes.
d. You must get a good (grape / wage) for the work you do.
e. It's nice to sit in the (shade / shave) on a sunny day.
f. I like to eat (cake / whale) at lunchtime.

**7** Change one letter in each word to make a new word.
Write the new words in your book. The first one has been done for you.

a.

| s | h | a | d | e |
|---|---|---|---|---|
| *s* | *p* | *a* | *d* | *e* |

b.

| s | h | a | m | e |
|---|---|---|---|---|
| | | | | |

c.
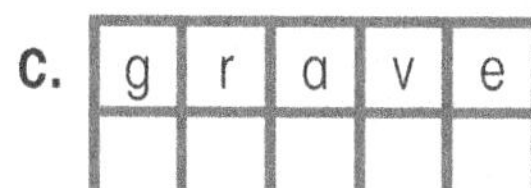


d.
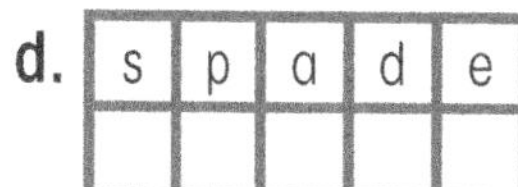


e.

| p | a | g | e |
|---|---|---|---|
| | | | |

f.
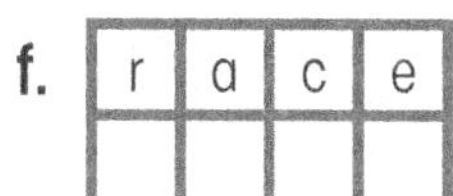


g.
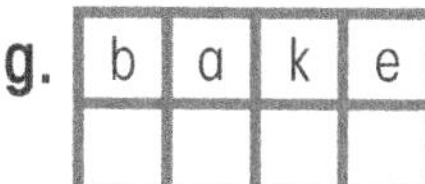


**8** Copy this crossword in your book. Write the correct word for each clue and find the mystery word.
Write the mystery word in a sentence in your book.

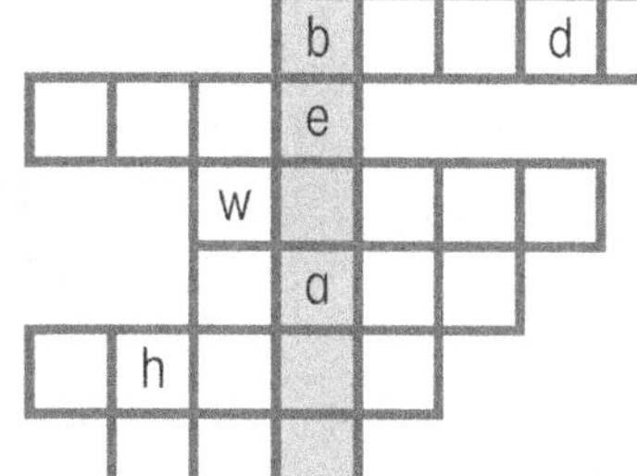


... the sharp part of a knife
... you bake it and put icing on it
... the largest sea mammal
... payment for work
... to scrape whiskers from your chin
... a kind of monkey

**RHYME time** › Copy this rhyme into your book and then ...

1. Circle all the words that end in '**–ake**'.
2. Draw a square around the words that end in '**–oke**'.
3. Find words inside other words, for example: d<u>rake</u> – rake.
   Find words inside: mistake, brake, awoke, goodness, made

*Billy-Jean Drake*
*Made a mistake —*
*She lifted her foot*
*Right off the brake!*

*Jonathon Stoke*
*One morning awoke*
*And told his Mum*
*A very rude joke.*
*For goodness sake — don't make THAT mistake!*

# WORD KNOWLEDGE › Contractions

**RULE**

**Contractions** are where two words are joined to make one word.
We use an **apostrophe** to show where a letter is left out, for example: *is* + *not* = *isn't*

**1** Choose contractions from the Contraction Box to match these words.
Write them in your book.

they are → ______ it is → ______ you are → ______
can not → ______ I am → ______ had not → ______

**Contraction B**

it's
can't
they're
I'm
you're
hadn't

**2** Write the two words that make up these contractions in your book.

she's here's isn't they're we're he's

**3** Write these contractions in sentences in your book.

don't it's can't I'm

## COMMON WORDS ›

**1** Choose words from the Spelling List to fill the gaps.
Write the complete sentences in your book.

a. Jenifa _ _ _ _ her pet dog a bath.
b. The monkey climbed _ _ _ _ from the tree to get to the ground.
c. I want a drink of _ _ _ _ _.
d. It is a long way _ _ _ _ Lae to Port Moresby.
e. The lost dog was _ _ _ _ _ in the bush.

Weekly Spelling List to be tested at the end of the week

**2** Find the opposites for these words in the Spelling List.
Write each pair of words in your book.

took lost up sleep

**Spelling LIST**

gave
found
from
down
water
game
frame
stage
cave
wake

**Writing activity › Cages for Wild Animals?**

- Some wild animals and birds are kept in cages. Do you think this is a good idea?
- Write what you think are the good and bad things about keeping wild animals in cages.

Unit 7

# FOCUS > Long vowel i–e

**RULE**

Remember, **long vowels** 'say' their name, for example, **i** – bride.
The '**e**' at the end of the word makes the vowel say its own name.

## Word LIST

| | |
|---|---|
| kite | spike |
| bite | stile |
| bride | grime |
| glide | pine |
| spice | site |
| hike | ice |
| bike | mime |
| smile | alive |
| pile | dime |
| rise | wide |
| wise | side |
| life | outside |
| wife | strike |
| crime | pike |
| slime | price |
| dine | nice |
| mine | guide |
| mile | like |
| quite | twine |
| ripe | nine |
| pipe | file |
| lice | swine |
| slide | |

**1** Copy this table into your book. Fill the gaps with '**i–e**' words to match the letter patterns. The first one has been done for you.

| –ite | –ice | –ike | –ile | –ine | –ime |
|---|---|---|---|---|---|
| *bite*<br>*quite*<br>*site*<br>*sprite*<br>*white* | | | | | |

**2** Write one word from each section of the table in a sentence in your book.

**3** Make words by connecting the letters in the boxes.
The first one has been done for you. Write the words in your book.

| | | |
|---|---|---|
| hi | se | *rise* |
| ri | fe | |
| wi | ze | |
| ki | de | |
| si | ce | |
| mi | te | |

| | | |
|---|---|---|
| ti | te | *bite* |
| bi | de | |
| di | se | |
| wi | ce | |
| ri | pe | |
| pi | de | |

**4** Choose words from the Word List to fill the gaps.
Write the complete sentences in your book.

a. The water turned to __ __ __ when it was very cold.
b. My father said that the __ __ __ __ __ of bread is too expensive.
c. I took a big __ __ __ __ out of the apple.
d. The wheel on the __ __ __ __ had a puncture.
e. Dani picked the __ __ __ __ bananas from the tree.
f. We went for a __ __ __ __ in the bush today.

**5** Choose a word from the Word List for each picture.
Write the words in alphabetical order in your book.

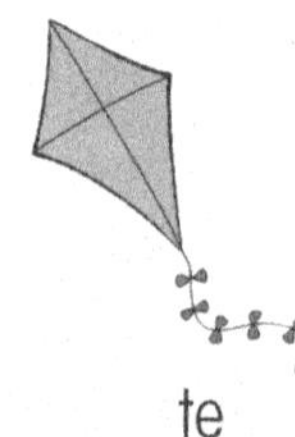

_ _ _de  _ _ke  _ _ _le  _ _te  _ce  _ _ _ne  _ _ne  _ _te

**6** Write the words above that begin with '**s–**' in sentences in your book.

**7** Find words from the Word List that have a similar meaning to these words.
Write the words in sentences in your book. The first one has been done for you.

to hit someone hard → *strike*  *The bully tried to strike the small boy.*

a word that describes fruit that is ready to be eaten →

a word that describes someone who knows and understands many things →

a woman on her wedding day →

another word for pigs →

to grip tightly with your teeth →

to float on the wind →

to have dinner →

a tube for carrying water →

**8** Copy this crossword in your book. Write the correct word for each clue and find the mystery word.
Write the mystery word in a sentence in your book.

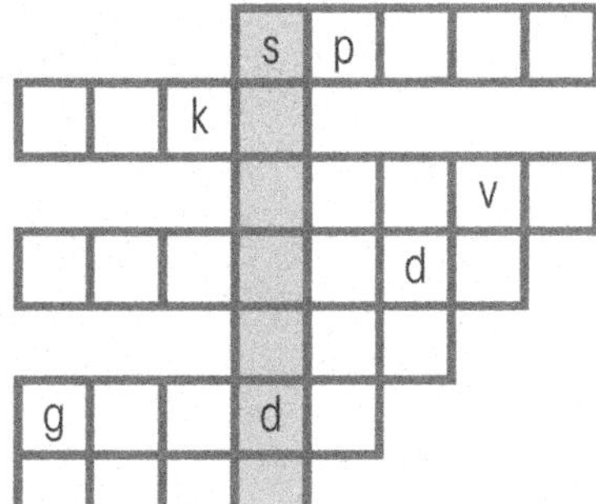


... very sharp with a point
... it has two wheels
... the opposite of dead
... the opposite of inside
... frozen water
... someone who shows people the way
... one less than ten

**RHYME time** › Copy this rhyme into your book and then ...

1. Circle all the words that end in '**–ide**'.
2. Find a word that ends in '**–ime**' and write it in a sentence.

*Run and hide,*
*Slip and slide.*
*Cake to eat,*
*Open wide!*

*Lemonade, freshly made.*
*Now's the time to party!*
*Slip and slide,*
*Jump and ride.*

*Games to play,*
*Two a side.*
*Time to make a birthday cake.*
*Now's the time to party!*

# WORD KNOWLEDGE › Nouns

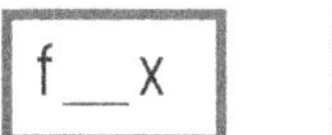

**Nouns** are the names for people, places, animals or things. For example: *horse, tree, stone, school, girl.*

**1** Fill the gaps by writing the nouns for the people, places, animals and things in this picture.

| f __ x | b __ y |
|---|---|
| ch __ __ __ __ __ | f __ nce |
| sh __ d | hou __ __ |
| b __ ck __ __ | d __ __ |

**2** Look around the playground at your school.
Write nouns in your book for ten things that you can see.

# COMMON WORDS ›

**1** Choose words from the Spelling List to fill the gaps.
Write the complete sentences in your book.

a. Simon __ __ __ first prize at the sing sing.
b. When you are __ __ __ __ __ you smile a lot.
c. We have our breakfast early in the __ __ __ __ __ __ __.
d. Letti and Amo like __ __ __ __ __ __ __ outside when school finishes.
e. Lani did not __ __ __ __ to go to the shops today.

Weekly Spelling List to be tested at the end of the week

**Spelling LIST**

won
morning
playing
want
happy
smile
quite
wide
like
file

**2** Find the opposites for these words in the Spelling List.
Write each pair of words in your book.

unhappy narrow dislike frown

## Writing activity › A Happy Time

- Write about a really happy time you had with your family. You can write about who was there, what you did, where you went, when it happened and why it was such a happy time.
- When you have finished, look back at your writing. Count how many nouns you used.

# Unit 8

## FOCUS > Long vowel o–e

**RULE**

Remember, **long vowels** 'say' their name, for example: **o** – j**o**ke.
The '**e**' at the end of the word makes the vowel say its own name.

**Word LIST**

| | |
|---|---|
| broke | poke |
| joke | smoke |
| home | prose |
| gnome | rose |
| nose | drone |
| hose | lone |
| doze | mope |
| froze | rope |
| bone | spoke |
| phone | stroke |
| cope | those |
| hope | chose |
| choke | stone |
| envelope | throne |
| dome | antelop |
| pose | slope |
| vote | elope |
| cone | note |
| lope | prone |

**1** Copy this table into your book. Fill the gaps with 'o–e' words to match the letter patterns. The first one has been done for you.

| –oke | –ose | –one | –ope |
|---|---|---|---|
| broke<br>joke<br>choke<br>spoke<br>stroke | | | |

**2** Write one word from each section of the table in a sentence in your book.

**3** Make words by connecting the letters in the boxes.
The first one has been done for you. Write the words in your book.

| | | |
|---|---|---|
| jo | pe | joke |
| vo | se | |
| lo | ke | |
| do | te | |
| ro | ne | |
| tho | ze | |

| | | |
|---|---|---|
| ho | ne | phone |
| fro | ke | |
| pho | me | |
| smo | ze | |
| cho | pe | |
| slo | se | |

**4** Choose a word from the Word List for each picture.
Write the words in alphabetical order in your book.

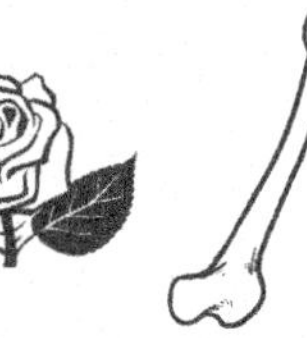
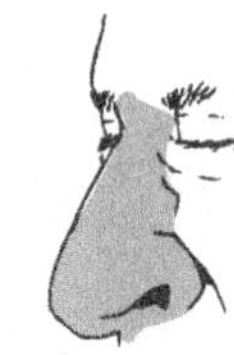
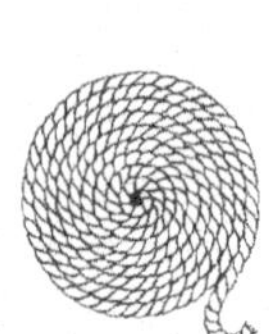

s__ __ke  r __se  b __ne  n __se  r __pe  h __se  p __ __ne  t __ __ __ne

**5** Write these words in alphabetical order in your book.

choke doze smoke slope note cope gnome spoke stroke throne those

**6** Choose the correct word. Write the words in complete sentences in your book.

a. Be careful not to (poke / joke) the stick in his eye.
b. The king sat on his (throne / home).
c. My teacher (broke / spoke) quietly to us.
d. We used a (nose / rope) to tow the car.
e. The (smoke / stone) in my shoe hurt my foot.
f. The (rose / bone) in Auntie's garden smelled beautiful.

**7** Use the words from the '**o–e**' Word Bank to solve these clues.
Write the words in your book.

a. you hold it to your ear to speak to someone →
b. it helps you see things that are far away →
c. you speak into it to make your voice louder →
d. it helps you see tiny things →
e. a doctor uses it to listen to your heart →
f. used in submarines to see above water →
g. it is a wild wind storm →
h. you hit it with small hammers to make music →

**O–E Word BANK**

telescope
telephone
periscope
microphone
cyclone
stethoscope
xylophone
microscope

**8** Choose one '**–ope**' word and one '**–one**' word from the '**o–e**' Word Bank.
Write them in sentences in your book.

**9** Add the letter '**e**' to these words to make new words.
Write both words in sentences in your book. The first one has been done for you.

a. hop → *hope* *The kangaroo can **hop** very high.*
*I **hope** you feel better tomorrow.*

b. not → c. mop → d. cod →

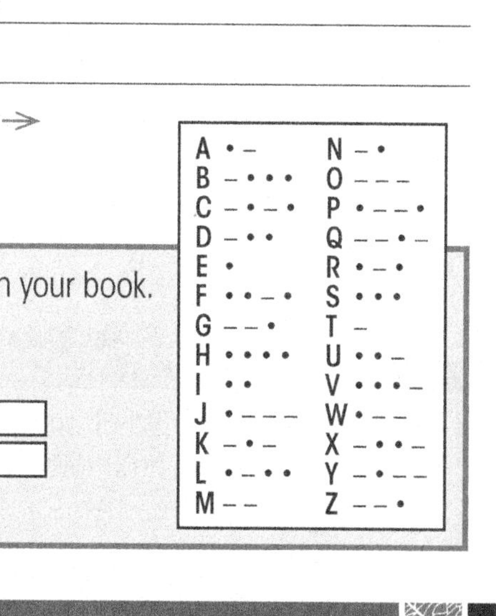

| | | | |
|---|---|---|---|
| A •– | N –• | | |
| B –••• | O ––– | | |
| C –•–• | P •––• | | |
| D –•• | Q ––•– | | |
| E • | R •–• | | |
| F ••–• | S ••• | | |
| G ––• | T – | | |
| H •••• | U ••– | | |
| I •• | V •••– | | |
| J •––– | W •–– | | |
| K –•– | X –••– | | |
| L •–•• | Y –•–– | | |
| M –– | Z ––• | | |

## Off the page

■ Use the Morse code to find these words. Write the words in sentences in your book.

| | | | | | | | | |
|---|---|---|---|---|---|---|---|---|
| a. | – | •••• | •–• | ––– | –• | • | | |
| b. | ––• | –• | ––– | –– | • | | | |
| c. | • | –• | •••– | • | •–•• | ––– | •––• | • |
| d. | •– | –• | – | • | •–•• | ––– | •––• | • |
| e. | ••–• | •–• | ––– | ––• | • | | | |

# WORD KNOWLEDGE › Singular and plural nouns

**RULE**

A **singular noun** is a word that describes **one** thing, for example: *boy, dog.*
A **plural noun** is a word that describes **more than one** thing.
Most of the time we add '**–s**' to the singular noun to make the plural, for example: *boys, dogs.*
We add '**–es**' to nouns that end in '**–ch**', '**–sh**', '**–x**', '**–s**', '**–ss**' or '**–zz**', for example: *boxes, branches, wishes.*
Some words are the same whether they are singular or plural, for example: *salmon, sheep.*

**1** Change these words from singular to plural. Write each one in a sentence in your book.

village girl tiger book

**2** Change these words from singular to plural. Write each one in a sentence in your book.

fox brush witch sandwich

**3** Write these words in sentences in your book in both the singular and plural forms.

trousers sheep scissors tongs

## COMMON WORDS ›

**1** Choose words from the Spelling List to fill the gaps.
Write the complete sentences in your book.

a. Tau didn't know _ _ _ _ to do next.
b. Sigi went out of the classroom, but then came back _ _ _ _ _.
c. I would _ _ _ _ to come to your party.
d. Gabbi's mother asked _ _ she had found her hat.
e. Joshua's father works _ _ a taxi driver.

**2** Fill the gaps to make these words from the Spelling List.
Write the words in your book.

a. f_ _z_ b. a_ _in c. s_ _p_
d. h_ _ _ e. l_v_

Weekly Spelling List to be tested at the end of the week

**Spelling LIST**

what
as
love
if
again
home
vote
slope
froze
joke

**Writing activity › Something Broke!**

■ Something broke. What was it? Was it a jar, a vase, your arm, a tree trunk?
Something broke down. Was it your car or a PMV?
Write about a time when something broke or broke down.

# FOCUS > Long vowel u–e

**✱ RULE**

Remember, **long vowels** 'say' their name, for example: **u** – f**u**se.
The '**e**' at the end of the word makes the vowel say its own name.

**Word LIST**

rude, nude, cute, flute, use, fuse, June, dune, rule, crude, brute, amuse, prune, exclude, include, chute, parachute, muse, ruse, accuse, confuse, intrude, lute, pollute, salute, excuse, misuse, abuse, tube, fumes, mule, duke, tune

**1** Copy this table into your book. Fill the gaps with '**a–e**' words to match the letter patterns. The first one has been done for you.

| –ude | –ute | –use |
|---|---|---|
| *rude*<br>*nude*<br>*crude*<br>*include*<br>*exclude* | | |

**2** Write one word from each section of the table in a sentence in your book.

**3** Find words from the Word List that have a similar meaning to these words. Write the words in sentences in your book. The first one has been done for you.

not very polite → *rude* *Don't be rude to your friends.*

strong smelling smoke or gas → ______

the sixth month of the year → ______

a long pipe that plays music → ______

to have no clothes on → ______

to make a place dirty and full of rubbish → ______

used to float to the ground from an aircraft → ______

**4** Choose words from the Word List to fill the gaps. Write the complete sentences in your book.

a. Sigi lit the f__ __ __ on the firecracker.
b. Tau had an e__ __ __ __ __ for being late, but the teacher didn't believe him.
c. It is a classroom r__ __ __ that we must not hit others.
d. The t__ __ __ in Michael's bike tyre had a puncture.
e. We all like to hear my father play a t__ __ __ on his flute.
f. The pilot floated down to the ground in his p__ __ __ __ __ __ __ __.

## 5 Copy these words into your book. Circle the odd one out.

| | | | | | |
|---|---|---|---|---|---|
| a. | rude | nude | July | June | rule |
| b. | fumes | mules | rules | tubes | flute |
| c. | include | exclude | intrude | latitude | pool |
| d. | smoke | pollute | fumes | fuse | use |
| e. | brute | cute | shoot | chute | lute |

## 6 Write as many words as you can in your book, using the magic word machines. Write the words in your book.

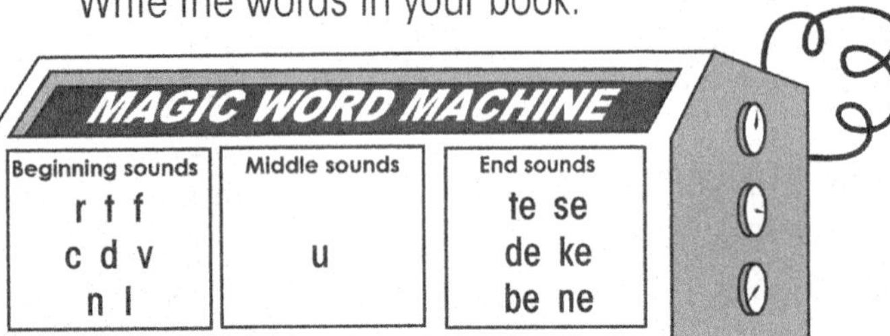


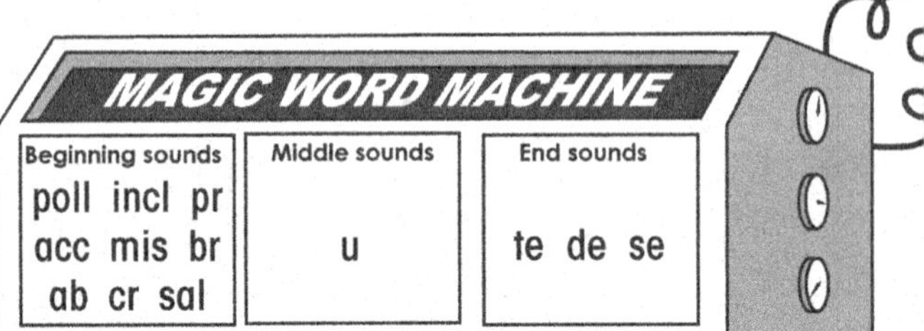


## 7 Find small words inside these words. Write each small word in a sentence in your book. The first one has been done for you.

cute → *cut* *He cut his finger with the bread knife.*

crude → ______ fuse → ______ use → ______

confuse → ______ amuse → ______ tube → ______

## 8 Copy this crossword in your book. Write the correct word for each clue and find the mystery word. Write the mystery word in a sentence in your book.

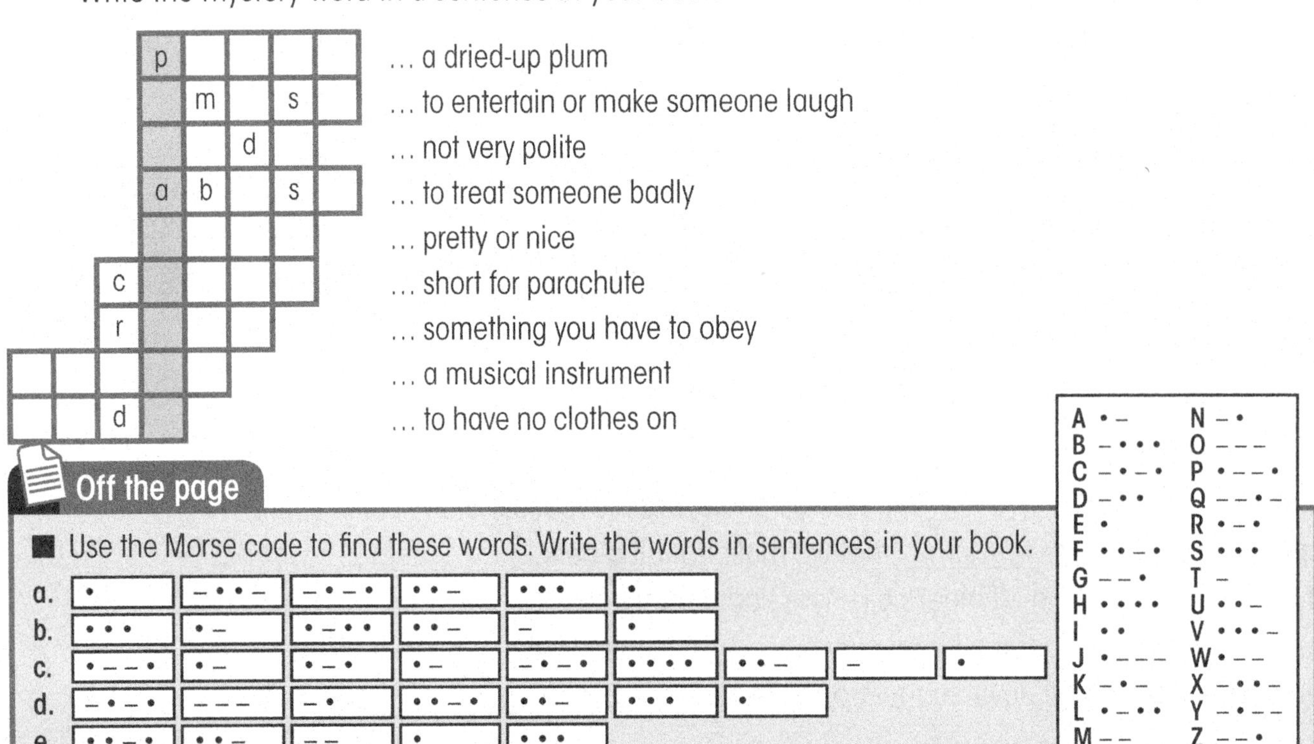

p _ _ _ _ … a dried-up plum

_ m _ s _ … to entertain or make someone laugh

_ _ d _ … not very polite

a b _ s _ … to treat someone badly

_ _ _ _ … pretty or nice

c _ _ _ _ … short for parachute

r _ _ _ … something you have to obey

_ _ _ _ … a musical instrument

_ _ d _ … to have no clothes on

### Off the page

■ Use the Morse code to find these words. Write the words in sentences in your book.

a. • | –••– | –•–• | ••– | ••• | •

b. ••• | •– | •–•• | ••– | – | •

c. •––• | •– | •–• | •– | –•–• | •••• | ••– | – | •

d. –•–• | ––– | –• | ••–• | ••– | ••• | •

e. ••–• | ••– | –– | • | •••

| | | | |
|---|---|---|---|
| A | •– | N | –• |
| B | –••• | O | ––– |
| C | –•–• | P | •––• |
| D | –•• | Q | ––•– |
| E | • | R | •–• |
| F | ••–• | S | ••• |
| G | ––• | T | – |
| H | •••• | U | ••– |
| I | •• | V | •••– |
| J | •––– | W | •–– |
| K | –•– | X | –••– |
| L | •–•• | Y | –•–– |
| M | –– | Z | ––•• |

# WORD KNOWLEDGE › Plural nouns

**RULE**

A **plural noun** is a word that describes more than one thing.
If a singular noun ends in a consonant and a '**–y**', we change the '**y**' to '**i**' and add '**–es**' to make the plural, for example: one *army* – two *armies*, one *canary* – two *canaries*.

**1** Circle the last consonant and the '**y**' in these words.
Change the '**y**' to '**i**' and add '**–es**' to make the plural words. Write them in your book.
The first one has been done for you.

| | | | |
|---|---|---|---|
| ci(ty) → *cities* | hobby → ______ | spy → ______ | pony → ______ |
| raspberry → ______ | story → ______ | puppy → ______ | factory → ______ |

**2** Change these singular nouns into plural nouns. Write them in sentences in your book.

party navy country baby

# COMMON WORDS ›

**1** Choose words from the Spelling List to fill the gaps.
Write the complete sentences in your book.

a. Everyone had a _ _ _ _ _ _ good time at the market.
b. We _ _ _ _ _ not get to school today.
c. Gabi went to the _ _ _ _ to buy some milk.
d. The girls are playing a _ _ _ _ of basketball at lunchtime.
e. I _ _ _ _ _ like to go to the sing sing tomorrow.

**2** Find rhyming words for these words from the Spelling List.
Write each pair of rhyming words in your book.

tame dune should chop refuse

**Spelling LIST**

game
really
could
shop
would
rule
amuse
tune
pollute
June

**Writing activity › Plural Sentences**

- Write sentences that use the plural of these words: story, lolly, city, hobby, strawberry. Make the plural nouns before you begin your story.

# FOCUS > Long vowels a–e, i–e

**Word BANK**

grade
bride
slime
stage
quite
grime
page
kite
lame
made
guide
wife
strike
nine
cave
fade
flame

**1** Choose the letter '**a**' or '**i**' to fill the gaps in these words from the Word Bank. Write the words in your book.

| | | | | | |
|---|---|---|---|---|---|
| fl__me | p__ge | gu__de | qu__te | k__te | gr__me |
| m__de | st__ge | sl__me | c__ve | gr__de | br__de |
| f__de | n__ne | w__fe | str__ke | | |

**2** Choose two '**a–e**' words and two '**i–e**' words. Write them in sentences in your book.

**3** Choose the correct word. Write the words in complete sentences in your book.

**a.** Sarah dropped the jar and it (brake / broke).
**b.** Be careful before you (dive / dine) into the river.
**c.** The (bride / guide) looked beautiful on her wedding day.
**d.** The teacher (gave / grade) the boy more homework.
**e.** I (smile / ride) my (kite / bike) to school every day.
**f.** The (while / whale) swam into the bay.
**g.** I (late / like) bananas that are very (ripe / wise).

**4** Copy this word grid in your book. Use the clues to find words. Write the words in your book. The first one has been done for you.

| | | | | | | | |
|---|---|---|---|---|---|---|---|
| s | p | a | d | e | | | … a tool with a long handle |
| o | u | | s | | | | … the opposite of inside |
| | | k | | | | | … it has two wheels and you ride it |
| | a | | | | | | … if something is not wild, it is …. |
| | l | | | | | | … fire that is shaped like a tongue |
| | w | | | | | | … another name for pigs |
| | | | | | | | … a very large sea mammal |
| | | | | | | | … an action that breaks the law |
| w | | | | | | | … someone who knows many things is … |

**5** Find rhyming words for these words. Write each pair of rhyming words in your book.

| | | | |
|---|---|---|---|
| game → ______ | grime → ______ | white → ______ | ride → ______ |
| knife → ______ | lake → ______ | like → ______ | blade → ______ |
| cage → ______ | fine → ______ | made → ______ | save → ______ |

# FOCUS > Long vowels o–e, u–e

**1** Choose the letter 'o' or 'u' to fill the gaps in these words from the Word Bank. Write the words in your book.

| | | | | |
|---|---|---|---|---|
| fr__ze | st__ne | r__de | gn__me | envel__pe |
| j__ke | sm__ke | c__te | am__se | br__te |
| f__se | J__ne | v__te | c__ne | parach__te |

**2** Choose two 'o–e' words and two 'u–e' words. Write them in sentences in your book.

**3** Choose the correct word. Write the words in complete sentences in your book.

a. Be careful that you don't breathe in the (fumes / bones).
b. Joshua (chose / those) to go home early.
c. The (lone / tune) he played on the (flute / fuse) was very happy.
d. Sigi told her mother that she would be (phone / home) for lunch.
e. Gabi threw a (hose / stone) and it (broke / joke) the window.
f. It is (rude / rule) to eat with your mouth full.
g. I saw the soldier (salute / pollute) to the captain.

**4** Copy this word grid in your book. Use the clues to find words. Write the words in your book. The first one has been done for you.

| | | | | | | | | | |
|---|---|---|---|---|---|---|---|---|---|
| s | t | o | n | e | | | | | … a small rock |
| m | | | | | | | | | … a cross between a donkey and a horse |
| a | n | | e | l | | | | | … an animal like a deer found in Africa |
| | | s | | | | | | | … a sweet smelling flower |
| p | | | a | | h | | | | … this is used to float to the ground from a plane |
| c | | n | f | | | | | | … to make someone puzzled |
| | | | | | | | | | … you use it to smell with |
| d | | n | | | | | | | … a mountain of sand in the desert |
| g | n | | | | | | | | … a kind of dwarf in fairytales |

**5** Find rhyming words for these words. Write each pair of rhyming words in your book.

| | | | | |
|---|---|---|---|---|
| froze → ______ | spoke → ______ | lure → ______ | use → ______ | bone → ______ |
| stone → ______ | tune → ______ | cube → ______ | note → ______ | broke → ______ |
| cube → ______ | doze → ______ | dune → ______ | drone → ______ | throne → ______ |
| nude → ______ | flute → ______ | poke → ______ | elope → ______ | excuse → ______ |

**Word BANK**

joke
stone
rude
parachute
gnome
fuse
amuse
vote
froze
lope
smoke
envelope
brute
tube
June
cute
cone
note
poke

Unit 11

## FOCUS > 'e' sound (as in 'meet' / 'meat')

**1** Choose the letters 'ee' or 'ea' to fill the gaps in these words from the Word List. Write the words in your book.

str__ __t  str__ __m  s__ __t  asl__ __p  wh__ __l  dr__ __m

scr__ __m  sp__ __d  wh__ __t  l__ __d  st__ __p  f__ __t

**✱ RULE**

Remember, a **homophone** is a word with the same sound as another word, but with different spelling and a different meaning, for example: *see* and *sea*.

**2** Read these words and write each one in your book with its meaning. The first one is done for you.

meat → *the flesh of an animal*

meet → *to come together with another person or people*

bean →   been →   sea →   see →

steal →   steel →   real →   reel →

**3** Can you find any more words in the Word List that sound the same but are spelt differently?

**HINT** There are eight more pairs of homophones in the Word List.

**4** Find words from the Word List to complete these rhyming puzzles. Write each pair of words in your book. The first one has been done for you.

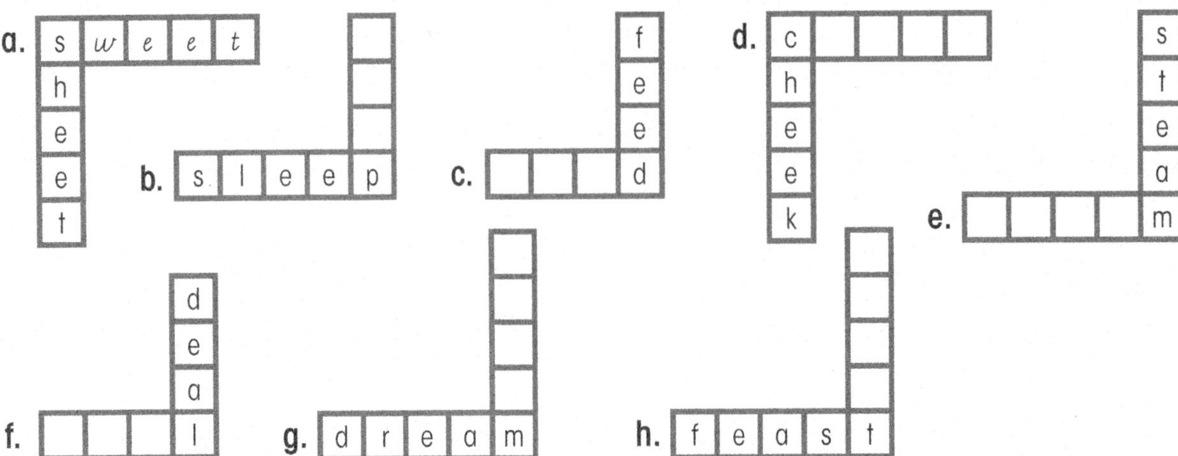


**Word LIST**

| | |
|---|---|
| beak | sheet |
| cream | speak |
| bee | steep |
| cheek | weak |
| peek | screar |
| feel | peak |
| street | strean |
| feast | weed |
| leak | week |
| seat | wheel |
| dream | wheat |
| flee | street |
| speed | creak |
| knee | real |
| neat | creek |
| meat | flea |
| wheat | beast |
| feet | steam |
| meet | team |
| lead | deep |
| leek | feat |
| reel | teem |
| cheap | cheep |
| sweet | leap |

**5** Use the beginning and ending sounds to write '**ee**' and '**ea**' words in your book.

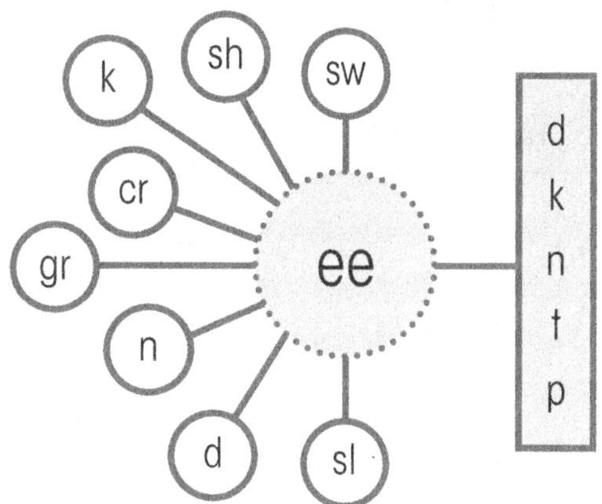


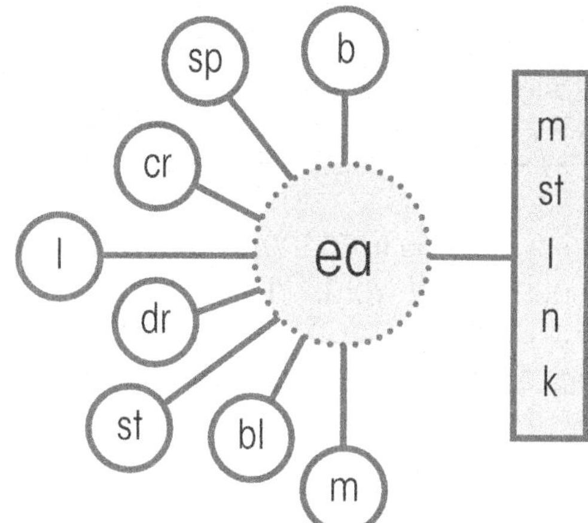


**6** Change one letter in each word to make a new word.
Write the new words in your book. The first one has been done for you.

**a.**

| s | t | r | e | a | m |
|---|---|---|---|---|---|
| *s* | *c* | *r* | *e* | *a* | *m* |

**b.**

| f | e | e | l |
|---|---|---|---|
| | | | |

**c.**

| f | e | a | s | t |
|---|---|---|---|---|
| | | | | |

**d.**

| c | h | e | e | p |
|---|---|---|---|---|
| | | | | |

**e.**

| h | e | a | t |
|---|---|---|---|
| | | | |

**7** Use the words from the Word Bank to fill the gaps. Write the complete sentences in your book.

**Word BANK**

clean sweep weed creek meet jeep street feed sleep

a. Joe must _ _ _ _ the chickens.
b. Joe must _ _ _ _ the garden.
c. Joe must _ _ _ _ _ his room.
d. Joe must _ _ _ _ _ the floor.
e. Joe must walk to the _ _ _ _ _ to wash his clothes.
f. Joe must _ _ _ _ his friend down the _ _ _ _ _ _ in the afternoon.
g. Joe must drive back in a _ _ _ _.
h. Joe must go to _ _ _ _ _ before nine o'clock.

**RHYME time ›** Copy this rhyme into your book and then ...

1. Circle all the '**ea**' words.
2. Choose three '**ea**' words and write them in sentences in your book.

*I scream, you scream,*
*We all scream*
*For ice cream.*
*I dream, you dream,*
*We all dream*
*For ice cream.*
*So if I scream,*
*And you dream,*
*Let's give the whole team*
*some ICE CREAM!*

# WORD KNOWLEDGE > Synonyms

**RULE**

A **synonym** is a word that means the **same** as another word.
For example, a synonym for *friend* is *mate*, a synonym for *small* is *little* and a synonym for *hot* is *warm*.

**1** Choose synonyms from the Synonym Box to match these words.
Write each pair of words in your book.

cold weep fast huge shiny torn dirty tiny

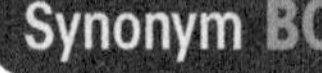

**Synonym BOX**

chilly
bright
swift
big
small
ripped
cry
filthy

**2** Copy these words into your book. Circle the odd one out.

| | | | | | | |
|---|---|---|---|---|---|---|
| a. | small | little | tiny | large | undersized | |
| b. | noisy | loud | rowdy | quiet | deafening | |
| c. | cry | weep | wail | laugh | sob | snivel |
| d. | run | scurry | race | trot | walk | sprint |

**3** Write the odd words out in sentences in your book.

## COMMON WORDS >

**1** Choose words from the Spelling List to fill the gaps.
Write the complete sentences in your book.

a. Amo ran _ _ _ _ the hill.
b. Lana _ _ _ _ _ her lost bracelet in the cupboard.
c. I want a drink of cold _ _ _ _ _.
d. The teacher _ _ _ _ everyone a new pencil.
e. Simon _ _ _ _ to the market yesterday.

**2** Write two words from the Spelling List that rhyme with '**see**'.

**Spelling LIST**

gave
found
went
down
water
speak
wheel
bee
sea
knee

**Writing activity > Danger in the Home**

- Make a list of some of the things in your home that are dangerous. Write about how you could keep your home safe. Make a safety poster about keeping your home safe.

## Unit 12

# FOCUS › 'o' sound (as in 'no' / 'coat' / 'grow')

**1** Choose the letters '**o**', '**oa**' or '**ow**' to fill the gaps in these words from the Word List. Write the words in your book.

| | | | | |
|---|---|---|---|---|
| gr__ __ | t__ __sted | s__ __k | als__ | c__ __ch |
| tomorr__ __ | yell__ __ | pill__ __ | b__ __s t | rainb__ __ |
| gr__ __n | __ __n | n__body | gh__st | hell__ |

**✻ RULE**

Remember, a **homophone** is a word with the same sound as another word, but with different spelling and a different meaning, for example: *so* and *sow*.

**2** Read these words and write each one in your book with its meaning. The first one is done for you.

so → *for that reason*　　　　sow → *put seeds in the ground*

groan →　　　grown →　　　road →　　　rode →

moan →　　　mown →　　　know →　　　no →

**3** Find words from the Word List to complete these rhyming puzzles. Write each pair of words in your book. The first one has been done for you.

a.
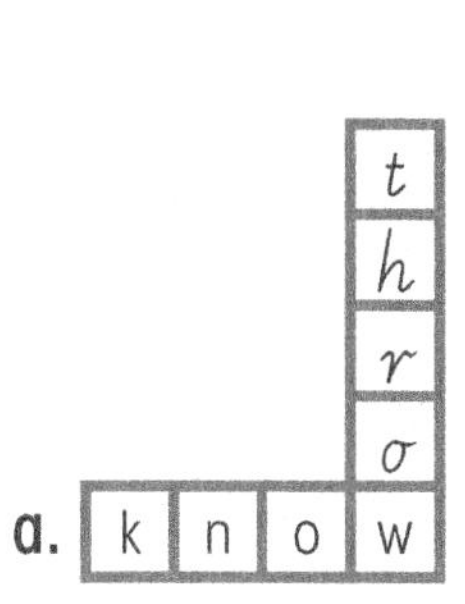


b.
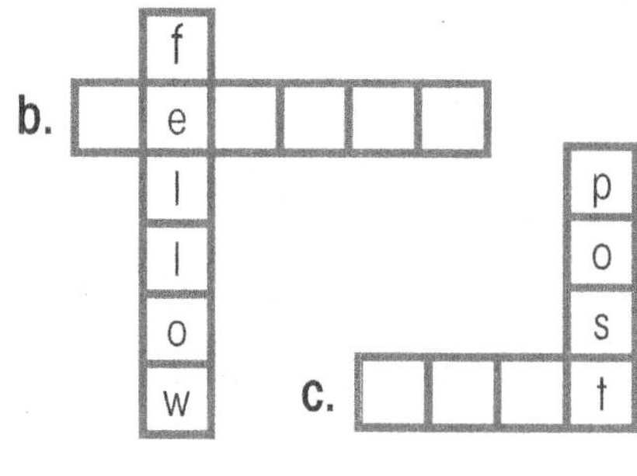


c.

d.
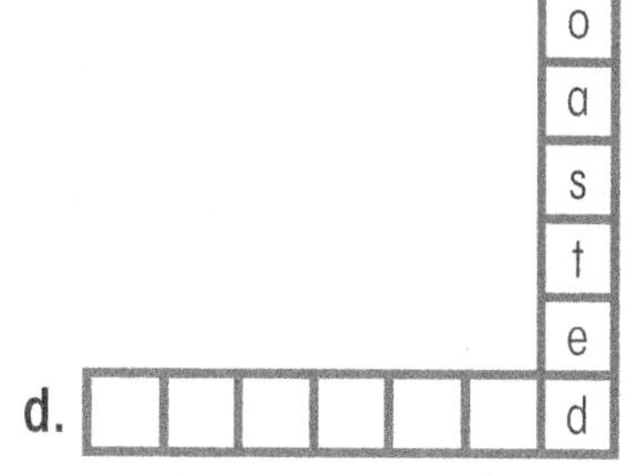


e.
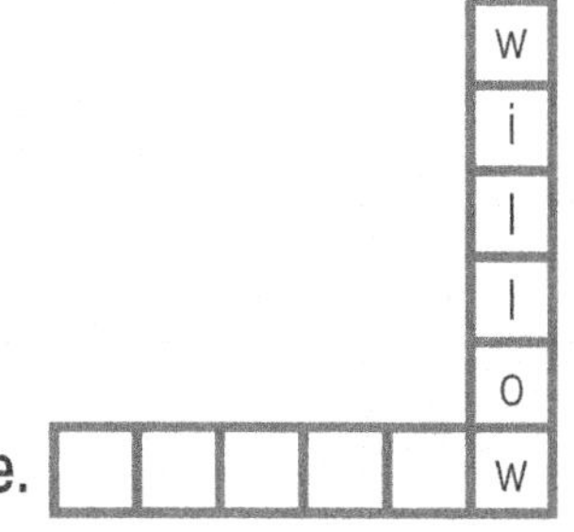


f.
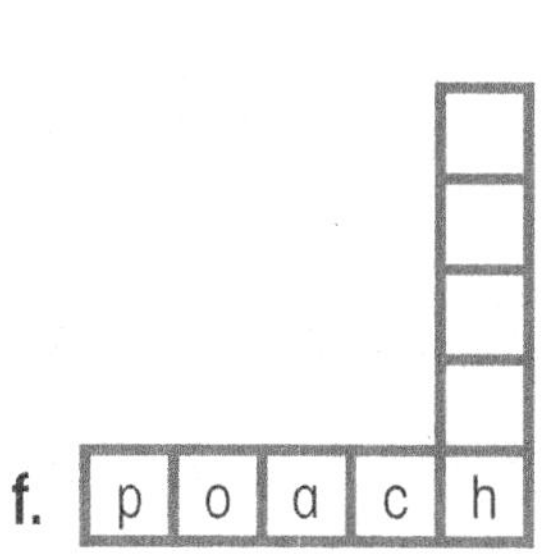


g. b a r r o w (down); a _ _ _ _ (across)

**Word LIST**

boat
goat
low
go
show
grow
coat
road
tow
blowing
no
load
crow
ago
foam
moan
groan
slow
also
own
soap
soak
piano
yellow
window
arrow
loaf
post
tomorrow
borrow
zero
rainbow
toast
hello
boast
coach
grown
pillow
groan
elbow
toasted
float
flow
boast
ghost
nobody
potato
boasted
poach
fellow
willow
tomato
most

**4** Use the beginning and ending sounds to write '**ow**' and '**oa**' words in your book.

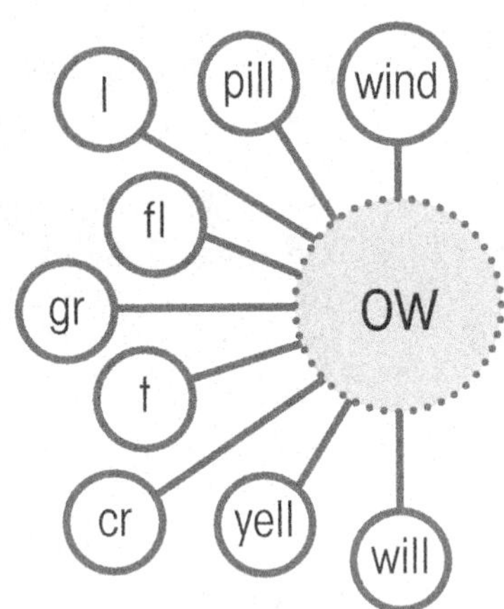


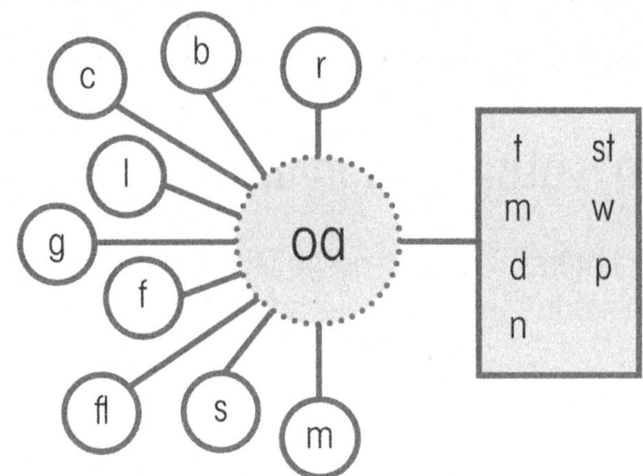


**5** Change one letter in each word to make a new word.
Write the new words in your book. The first one has been done for you.

a.

| r | o | a | d |
|---|---|---|---|
| *t* | *o* | *a* | *d* |

b.

| b | o | a | s | t |
|---|---|---|---|---|
| | | | | |

c.

| w | i | l | l | o | w |
|---|---|---|---|---|---|
| | | | | | |

d.

| b | o | a | t |
|---|---|---|---|
| | | | |

e.

| s | l | o | w |
|---|---|---|---|
| | | | |

f.

| g | r | o | w |
|---|---|---|---|
| | | | |

**6** Find small words inside these words. Write each small word in a sentence in your book.
The first one has been done for you.

flow → *low* *The plane flew low over the building.*

rainbow → ______ grown → ______ toasted → ______

nobody → ______ blowing → ______

**RHYME time** › Copy this rhyme into your book and then ...

1. Circle all the '**oa**' words.
2. Why did the goats get on the boat?
3. Why didn't they get there?
4. Draw a picture with labels that shows what happened to the goats.

*The goats*
*Got on the boat*
*To cross the moat*
*And eat the oats*
*On the other side of the hill.*

*BUT ...*
*The goats didn't get there ...*
*Why?*
*The boat didn't float!*

# WORD KNOWLEDGE > Antonyms

**RULE**

An **antonym** is a word that means the **opposite**.
For example, the antonym of *big* is *little* and the antonym of *hot* is *cold*.

**1** Choose antonyms from the Antonym Box to match these words.
Write each pair of words in your book.

first big up hot on strong happy light clean

**Antonym BOX**

dirty sad
dark weak
off little
cold last
down

**2** Change the underlined words in these sentences to opposites.
Write the new sentences in your book. The first one is done for you.

a. The drink is hot. *The drink is cold.*
b. The milk bottle is full.
c. I found a silver bracelet.
d. John's dad is very strong.
e. We will be early for school.
f. The small cat attacked the dog.

**3** Change these words to opposites. Write them in sentences in your book.

fat tall wrong open smooth dark

## COMMON WORDS >

**1** Choose words from the Spelling List to fill the gaps.
Write the complete sentences in your book.

a. We will go to the shop to buy some _ _ _ _ for dinner.
b. The _ _ _ _ girl drank the milk from a bottle.
c. We are going to _ _ _ _ _ the boys play basketball.
d. Sila's dad parked the car _ _ the side of the road.
e. The parents _ _ _ _ _ the baby Joseph.

**Spelling LIST**

by
food
named
baby
watch
know
ghost
rainbow
nobody
slowcoach

**2** Write the words from the Spelling List with a silent '**h**' and a silent '**k**' in your book.

**3** Write the three compound words from the Spelling List in your book.

**Writing activity > When I Was Bad ...**

- Write about a time when you were really bad at school or at home.
  Did you get into trouble? Did you try to make an excuse? What happened next?

Unit 13

# FOCUS > 'u' sound (as in 'glue' / 'screw')

**1** Choose the letters '**ue**' or '**ew**' to fill the gaps in these words from the Word List. Write the words in your book.

| | | | | | |
|---|---|---|---|---|---|
| st__ __ | d__ __ | val__ __ | cl__ __ | aven__ __ | scr__ __ |
| untr__ __ | dr__ __ | corkscr__ __ | j__ __el | stat__ __ | kn__ __ |

**✱ RULE**

Remember, a **homophone** is a word with the same sound as another word, but with different spelling and a different meaning, for example: *dew* and *due*.

**2** Read these words and write each one in your book with its meaning. The first one is done for you.

flue → *The smoke went up the chimney flue.*

flew → *The bird flew over the treetops.*

blue → ______ blew → ______

new → ______ knew → ______

dew → ______ due → ______

**3** Find words from the Word List that have a similar meaning to these words. Write the words in sentences in your book. The first one has been done for you.

to keep biting food while you eat it → *chew* *I chew my food before I swallow it.*

a model of a person made in stone → ______ a very beautiful stone → ______

a tool used to get a cork out of a bottle → ______ not true → ______

a road with trees along each side → ______ a tool for turning a screw → ______

**4** Choose the correct word. Write the words in complete sentences in your book.

a. The wind (knew / blew) the tree right over.
b. We used some (glue / clue) to stick the paper on the wall.
c. Mum made a pot of (glue / stew) for dinner.
d. We painted the front door (blew / blue).
e. It is not (true / blew) that Lae is the largest city in the country.
f. My grandma bought a (new / glue) bilum at the market.
g. Make sure you (stew / screw) the lid on the jar.

**Word LIST**

blew
chew
nephew
true
stewing
blue
screw
grew
new
due
queue
brew
knew
value
flue
clue
stew
flew
tissue
untrue
drew
reuse
few
jewel
view
statue
avenue
dew
corkscrew
screwdriver
chewing
screwed
rescue

**5** Use the beginning and ending sounds to write '**ew**' and '**ue**' words in your book.

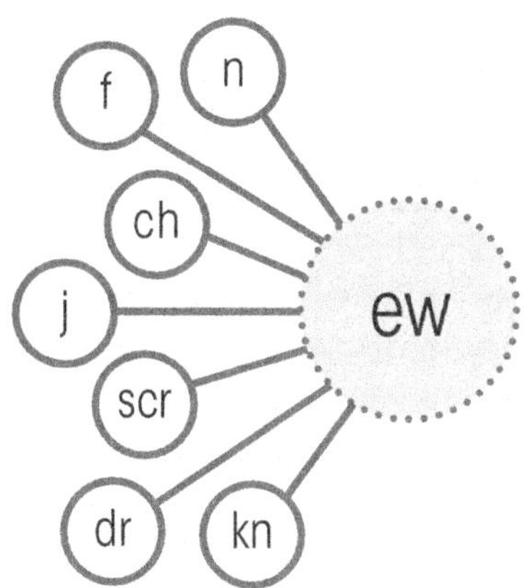


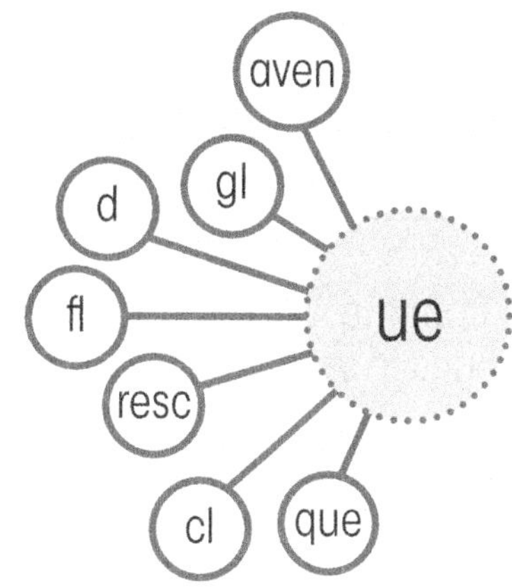


**6** Copy this table into your book. Fill the gaps to complete the table.

| screw | | | | brew |
|---|---|---|---|---|
| screws | views | | | |
| screwed | | chewed | | brewed |
| screwing | viewing | | stewing | |

**7** Choose words from the Word List to fill the gaps.
Write the complete sentences in your book.

a. The lifesavers had to _ _ _ _ _ _ some children from the water.
b. The bamboo shoots _ _ _ _ very quickly when the rain came.
c. He used the _ _ _ _ to solve the crossword puzzle.
d. It was so cold this morning there was _ _ _ on the ground.
e. We had to wait in a long _ _ _ _ _ before we bought the tickets.
f. It was a beautiful _ _ _ _ from the top of the mountain.
g. Dad bought Silas a _ _ _ bike for his birthday.

## Off the page

**What Am I?**
When you have found the answers, choose three more words of your own and write clues for them. Ask your friend to guess what the words are.

| *I am sparkling.*<br>*I am very precious.*<br>*I am a ________.* | *I am made of metal.*<br>*I undo corks.*<br>*I am a ________.* | *I am a boy.*<br>*I have an uncle.*<br>*I am a ________.* | *I am made of meat.*<br>*I am made of vegetables.*<br>*I am a ________.* |
|---|---|---|---|

# WORD KNOWLEDGE › Adjectives

**RULE**

An **adjective** is a word that describes a noun, for example: a *red* rose, a *big* balloon.
In these examples, '*red*' and '*big*' are adjectives; '*rose*' and '*balloon*' are nouns.

**1** Choose the best adjective from the Adjective Box to describe each noun.
Write the adjectives and nouns in your book.

house tomato star baby hair cat day giraffe

**Adjective BOX**

sunny tall
bright fluffy
brick tiny
ripe curly

**2** Write these sentences in your book.
Circle the adjectives in the sentences.

a. Leti is a fast runner.
b. John caught a big fish today.
c. The hungry boy ate the chocolate cake.
d. That big black dog ran away.
e. Kina is a happy girl.
f. The little pig ran away.

# COMMON WORDS ›

**1** Choose words from the Spelling List to fill the gaps.
Write the complete sentences in your book.

a. When it stopped raining we were allowed to go _ _ _ _ _ _ _ to play.
b. The teacher was _ _ _ _ today so some children were naughty.
c. There are two children and two adults in our _ _ _ _ _ _.
d. My _ _ _ _ _ _ _ _ _ food is ice cream.
e. Our dad _ _ _ to go to work early in the morning.

**Spelling LIST**

outside
away
favourite
has
family
flew
true
corkscrew
screwdriver
clue

**2** Find smaller words in these compound words.
Write them in sentences in your book.

corkscrew screwdriver

**Writing activity › Title?**

- How does food taste? Use these adjectives in sentences in your book to describe how different foods taste – sour, sweet, spicy, sickly.
- What is your favourite food? Describe it and say why you like it.

# Unit 14

## FOCUS › 'i' sound (as in 'fly' / 'child')

**1** Choose the letters 'i' or 'y' to fill the gaps in these words from the Word List. Write the words in your book.

| | | | | | |
|---|---|---|---|---|---|
| sk__ | f__nd | unk__nd | dragonfl__ | beh__nd | sl__ |
| Jul__ | b__ | cl__mb | gr__nd | multipl__ | m__nd |
| butterfl__ | ch__ld | cr__ | b__c__cle | | |

**✱ RULE**

Some words have the **same spelling** but a **different meaning**, for example: *fly* (a small insect with wings) and *fly* (to move through the air using wings).

**2** Read the meanings for these words. Write each one in a sentence in your book. The first pair has been done for you.

behind (at the back or hidden) → *She is behind the tree.*

behind (a person's bottom) → *He kicked me on the behind.*

blind (not able to see) →

blind (a cover for a window) →

try (a score in rugby) →

try (to work hard at something) →

kind (friendly, helpful) →

kind (a sort or type of thing) →

**3** Find words from the Word List to complete these rhyming puzzles. Write each pair of words in your book.

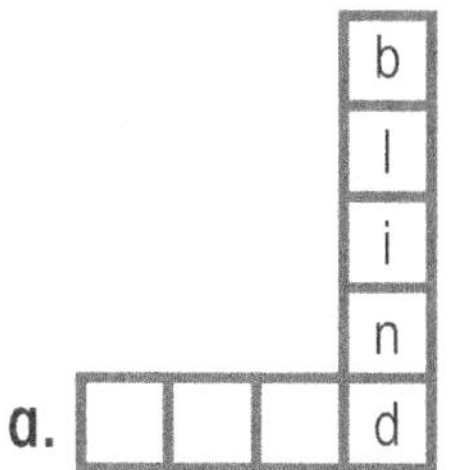


b. f l y

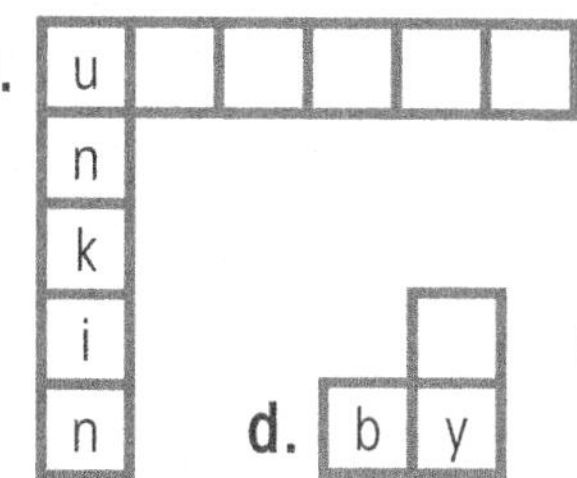


d. b y

e. w i n d

f. c h i l d

**4** Choose the correct word. Write the words in complete sentences in your book.

a. The small (wild / child) was playing in the sand.
b. The grandmother took her (grandchild / butterfly) to the sing sing.
c. If you want to stay (dry / fly), take an umbrella.
d. Colitha helped the (blind / mind) man across the road.
e. If you (multiply / unwind) two by three you will get six.

**Word LIST**

sky
my
blind
mind
by
find
dry
cry
kind
grind
behind
try
fry
unkind
unwind
fly
sly
July
wild
child
climb
grandchild
butterfly
dragonfly
trial
riot
multiply
bicycle
crying
trying

**5** Use the beginning and ending sounds to write 'i' and 'y' words in your book.

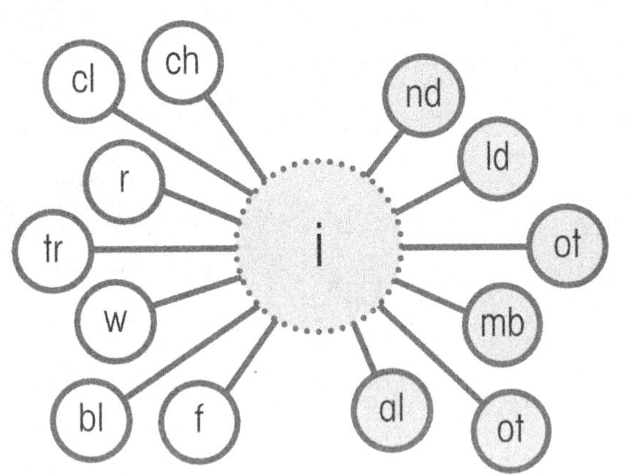


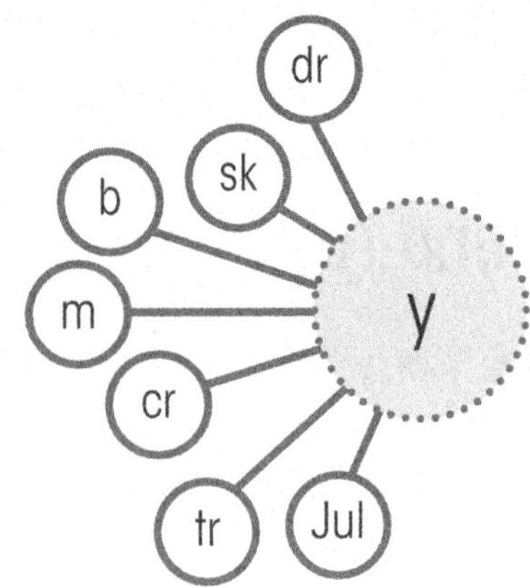


**6** Find small words inside these words. Write each small word in a sentence in your book. The first one has been done for you.

trying → *try* *I will try my best today.*

behind → ______ unkind → ______ grandchild → ______ butterfly → ______

dragonfly → ______ crying → ______ find → ______

**7** Use words from the Word List to complete these sentences. Write the complete sentences in your book.

**a.** Rina likes to _ _ _ _ _ the tree near our house.

**b.** You must not get _ _ _ _ _ _ in your schoolwork.

**c.** Dad likes to _ _ _ the fish in a pan.

**d.** Can you _ _ _ _ my lost wallet?

**e.** It would be _ _ _ _ _ _ _ to stand on a cat's tail.

**f.** The month that comes after June is _ _ _ _.

**g.** The criminal was put on _ _ _ _ _ for robbing the bank.

## Off the page

**What Am I?**

When you have found the answers, choose three more words of your own and write clues for them. Ask your friend to guess what the words are.

| | | | |
|---|---|---|---|
| *I am blue.*<br>*I am up above you.*<br>*The sun is here.*<br>*I am the ______.* | *I am an insect.*<br>*I can fly.*<br>*I have large wings.*<br>*I am a ______.* | *I have two wheels.*<br>*You can ride me.*<br>*I have brakes.*<br>*I am a ______.* | *I am little.*<br>*I am young.*<br>*I am a son or daughter.*<br>*I am a ______.* |

# WORD KNOWLEDGE > Adjectives

**RULE**

Remember, an **adjective** is a word that describes a noun, for example: It was a *beautiful* sunset. In this example, '*beautiful*' is an adjective. It describes the noun '*sunset*'.

**1** Find an adjective to describe these nouns. Write the adjectives and nouns in your book.

animal banana woman bag hen axe

**2** Write these adjectives and nouns in sentences of your own in your book.

| | | | | | |
|---|---|---|---|---|---|
| a. | small baby | b. | huge pumpkin | c. | old spade |
| d. | green beans | e. | big bilum | f. | hot chilli |

**3** Write this paragraph in your book. Circle the adjectives.

My mum has curly hair. She has brown eyes and a smiley mouth. When she goes out, she likes to wear a blue sarong and leather sandals. She lives in a tall house with long stilts. She has a loud laugh and she loves us. She gives me the best hugs.

# COMMON WORDS >

**1** Choose words from the Spelling List to fill the gaps.
Write the complete sentences in your book.

a. When it is _ _ _ _ _ time, we all go out to play.
b. Mum and Dad go to the _ _ _ _ _ to buy food on the weekend.
c. Yesterday a _ _ _ came to our house to fix our taps.
d. When I _ _ _ _ _ _ at the dog it barked at me.
e. Our school played a _ _ _ _ _ _ _ _ match last week.

**Spelling LIST**

lunch
man
shops
football
looked
unkind
unwind
climb
butterfly
multiply

**2** Write the opposite of these words in your book. kind wind

**3** Find a word in the Spelling List with the silent letter '**b**'.
Write it in a sentence in your book.

**Writing activity > My Dad**

- Write a paragraph about your dad. Use some adjectives to describe what he looks like and what he likes to do. Don't forget to describe how he helps the family and how he looks after you.

# Unit 15

## Revision

# FOCUS > Long 'e', 'o' sounds

**1** Copy these tables. Write words from Word Bank ① into the correct box.

Add two words of your own to the correct box.

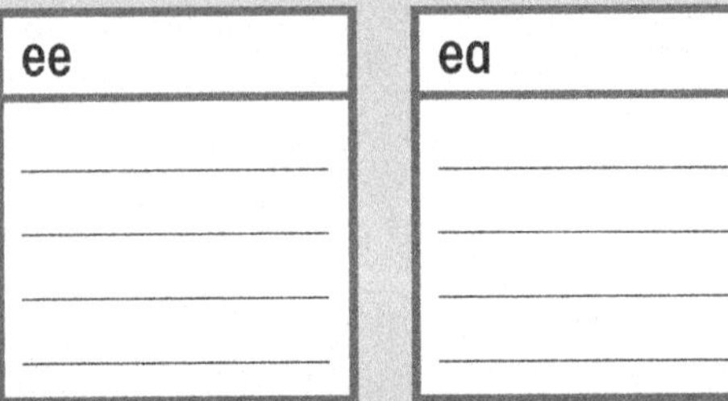

**2** Write each of these words in a sentence in your book to show its meaning.

| sea | peak | flee | meat | week | creak |
|---|---|---|---|---|---|
| see | peek | flea | meet | weak | creek |

**3** Add '**–ing**' to these words to form new words. Write them in sentences in your book.

read steam speed lead speak

**4** There are eight words in Word Bank ① that begin with the letter '**s**'. Write them in your book in alphabetical order.

**5** Copy these tables. Write words from Word Bank ② into the correct box.

Add two words of your own to the correct box.

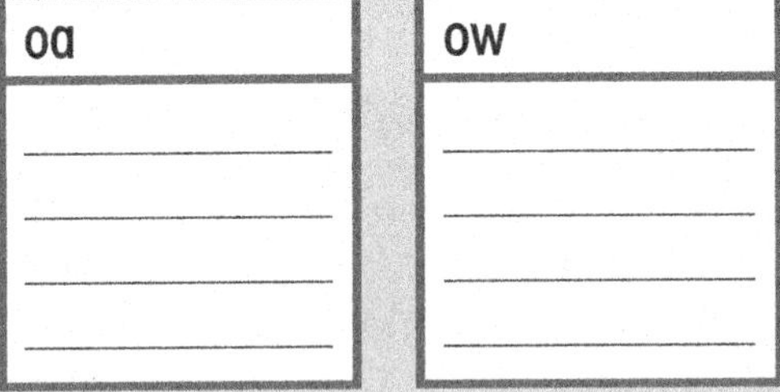

**6** Write each of these words in a sentence in your book to show its meaning.

| road | know | sow | moan | groan |
|---|---|---|---|---|
| rode | no | so | mown | grown |

**7** Add '**–ed**' to these words to form new words. Write them in sentences in your book.

tow boast own glow snow

### Word BANK ①

knee, east, read, green, seat, cheek, stream, steam, speed, weakness, bee, cheeky, meat, lead, dreaming, flee, scream, team, work, bee, sheep, screamed, weak, speak, need

### Word BANK ②

go, flowing, moan, tow, tomato, groan, boat, no, fellow, goat, grown, snow, glow, mow, road, boast, rode, know, yellow, ago, grow, tomorrow, elbow, potato, float, pillow, own

# FOCUS > Long 'u', 'i' sounds

**1** Copy these tables. Write words from Word Bank ③ into the correct box.

Add two words of your own to the correct box.

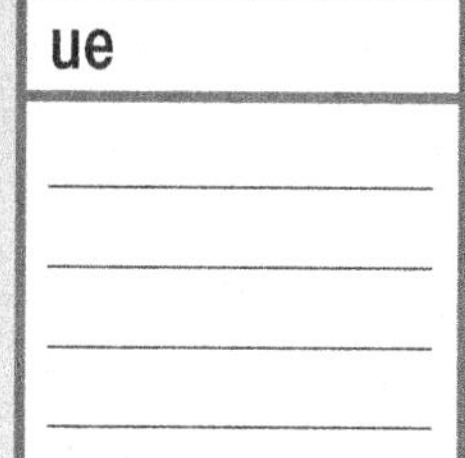

| ew |
|---|
| |
| |
| |
| |

**Word BANK ③**

| | |
|---|---|
| clue | grew |
| stew | value |
| flew | view |
| tissue | statue |
| blew | avenue |
| chew | corkscrew |
| stewing | screwdriver |
| screw | chewing |
| new | brew |
| due | jewel |
| screwed | rescue |
| dew | queue |
| blue | |

**2** Write each of these words in a sentence in your book to show its meaning.

| | | | |
|---|---|---|---|
| flue | new | blue | dew |
| flew | knew | blew | due |

**3** Add '–ing' to these words to form new words. Write them in sentences in your book.

stew chew view screw

**4** There are six words in Word Bank ③ that begin with the letter '**s**'. Write them in your book in alphabetical order.

**5** Copy these tables. Write words from Word Bank ④ into the correct box.

Add two words of your own to the correct box.

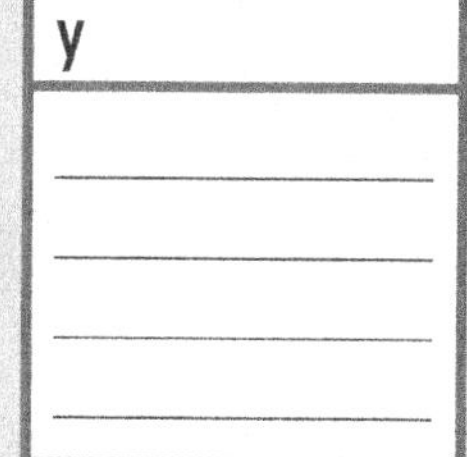

**Word BANK ④**

| | |
|---|---|
| sky | fry |
| trying | climb |
| my | kind |
| blind | unwind |
| dry | grind |
| mind | multiply |
| behind | child |
| by | fly |
| bicycle | sly |
| cry | unkind |
| find | butterfly |

**6** Copy these words into your book. Circle the odd one out.

| | | | | | |
|---|---|---|---|---|---|
| **a.** | groan | moan | behind | float | goat |
| **b.** | sky | fly | try | my | sty |
| **c.** | find | wind | kind | try | grind |
| **d.** | flow | grow | tow | butterfly | sow |
| **e.** | clue | value | queue | blind | avenue |
| **f.** | chew | multiply | grew | crew | few |

**7** There are eight words in Word Bank ④ that end in '**–ind**'. Write them in your book in alphabetical order.

# Unit 16

## FOCUS > 'a' sound (as in 'rain' / 'pray')

**Word LIST**

bail, fail, bay, day, main, pain, gay, hay, maid, laid, lay, may, day, faint, paint, pay, ray, jail, rain, paid, saint, play, mail, nail, pail, play, pray, slay, stain, vain, brain, chain, raid, quaint, pray, rail, chain, spray, stray, plain, sprain, sail, tail, snail, stay, sway, tray

**1** Choose the letters '**ai**' or '**ay**' to fill the gaps in these words from the Word List. Write the words in your book.

| | | | | | |
|---|---|---|---|---|---|
| str__ __ | t__ __l | p__ __ | str__ __n | m__ __d | p__ __l |
| br__ __n | st__ __ | r__ __n | sn__ __l | s__ __l | h__ __ |

**2** Choose a word from the Word Bank to complete these sentences.

**Word BANK**

train snail rails brain play Friday trail way
spray stain rain clay paint tray paid yesterday

a. I would love to ride on a t__ __ __ __. It would go very fast along the r__ __ __ __.
b. The sn__ __ __ doesn't move very fast.
c. We like to p__ __ __ football every d__ __.
d. The bush tr__ __ __ led all the w__ __ up to the mountains.
e. Mum used a sp__ __ __ to remove the st__ __ __ on my new dress.
f. The heavy r__ __ __ made the soil turn into clay.
g. He asked his mother if he could s__ __ __ home today.
h. Today I p__ __ __ two kina for a book.

**3** Find words from the Word List to complete these rhyming puzzles. Write each pair of words in your book.

**4** Find small words inside these words. Write each small word in a sentence in your book. The first one has been done for you.

Saturday → *day* *Tomorrow is the day we go to the sing sing.*

brain → ______ mainly → ______ betray → ______

sailor → ______ railway → ______ unchain → ______

**✱ RULE**

Remember, a **homophone** is a word with the same sound as another word, but with different spelling and a different meaning, for example: *see* and *sea*.

**5** Read these words and write each one in a sentence in your book to show its meaning. The first pair is done for you.

main → *The man walked through the main gate to get to the building*

mane → *The male lion had a very large mane.*

pain → pane → maid → made →

sail → sale → pale → pail →

tale → tail →

**6** Choose the correct word. Write the complete sentences in your book.

a. Wheat is a (grain / gray) that is used to make bread.
b. Mum will (brain / braid) my hair on the weekend.
c. The old lady couldn't walk and looked very (frail / vain).
d. The (spray / stray) dog was chasing the cars on the road.
e. I like to eat (slain / plain) sweet biscuits.

**7** Copy this table into your book. Fill the gaps to complete the table.

| fail | play | | | | paint |
|---|---|---|---|---|---|
| fails | | prays | | sways | |
| failed | | prayed | | | |
| failing | | | staying | | |

**Off the page**

■ **What Am I?**
When you have found the answers, choose three more words of your own and write clues for them. Ask your friend to guess what the words are.

*I live in a shell.*
*I move very slowly.*
*I am a ______.*

*I am a liquid.*
*I come from the sky.*
*I am ______.*

*I run on rails.*
*I carry people.*
*I am a ______.*

*I am in your head.*
*I think.*
*I am a ______.*

# WORD KNOWLEDGE › Past tense verbs

**RULE**

A **verb** is an *action* word that tells us what someone or something is doing, for example: *run, jump, cry, bark, laugh.*
If an **action** has **already happened**, you use the **past tense** of the verb.
Past tense verbs end in '**–ed**', for example: Yesterday I *kick**ed*** the football.

**1** Choose the correct verb. Write the complete sentence in your book.

a. I like to (sing / buy / look) at the concert.
b. Leila can (cry / hop / laugh) on one leg.
c. Please (eat / lick / cut) the bread straight.
d. The fielder (threw / sat / run) the ball to the wicketkeeper.

**2** Add '–ed' to change the verbs in these sentences into the past tense. Write the complete sentences in your book.

a. Yesterday I walk__ __ with my friends.
b. Last night I talk__ __ to my mother.
c. Last week I walk__ __ through the bush.
d. This morning I play__ __ basketball.
e. This evening I turn__ __ on the radio.

**3** Write these words in sentences of your own in your book.

laughed grunted sailed

## COMMON WORDS ›

**1** Choose words from the Spelling List to fill the gaps. Write the complete sentences in your book.

a. I __ __ __ __ __ __ to play outside, but the teacher said, "No."
b. Dad __ __ __ __ his wallet at the market.
c. The children at our school play football in the __ __ __ __ __ __ __ __ __ __.
d. Leti is going to __ __ __ __ __ a picture of her friend.
e. I will __ __ __ to find my shoes before I go outside to play.

Weekly Spelling List to be tested at the end of the week

**Spelling LIST**

wanted
bike
playground
lost
need
paint
sprain
try
pain
saint

**2** Write the compound word from the Spelling List in your book.

**3** Write the smaller words in the compound word in sentences in your book.

**Writing activity › An Accident**

- Write about a time when you had an accident or saw an accident. Remember to include some past tense verbs in your recount, for example: crashed, tripped, bounced, shouted.

# Unit 17

## FOCUS › 'ear' sound (as in 'cheer' / 'hear')

**1** Choose the letters '**eer**' or '**ear**' to fill the gaps in these words from the Word List. Write the words in your book.

b__ __ __   y__ __ __   n__ __ __   d__ __ __   s__ __ __

p__ __ __   qu__ __ __   cl__ __ r   r__ __ __

**2** Choose a word from the Word Bank to complete these sentences.

**Word BANK**

beer spear clear deer year cheer engineer near

a. There were many ______ in the zoo.
b. The day was very ______ so we went for a bush walk.
c. The bushman threw his ______ at the cuscus in the tree.
d. ______ is an alcoholic drink.
e. I will be starting Grade 6 next ______.
f. We will ______ on our football team at the game.
g. I would like to become an ______ when I grow up.
h. We live ______ a busy highway.

**3** Find words from the Word List to complete these rhyming puzzles. Write each pair of words in your book.

a. d _ a _ / _ e _

b. 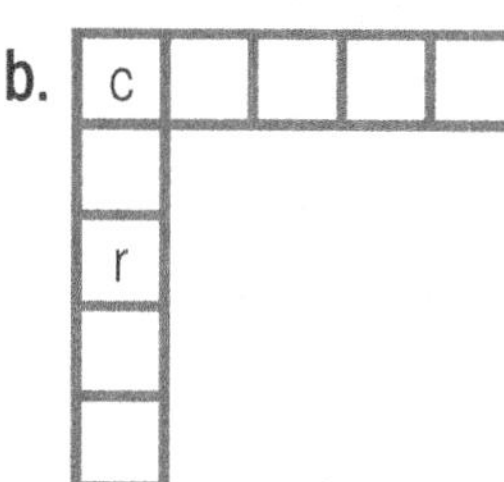

c. 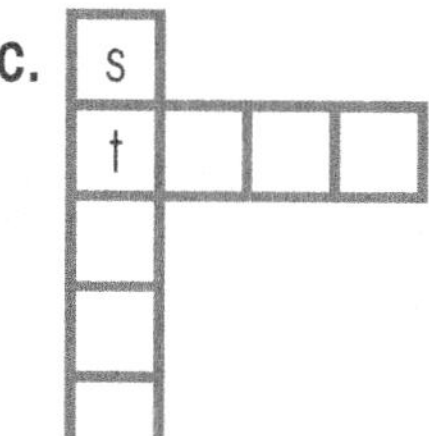

d. 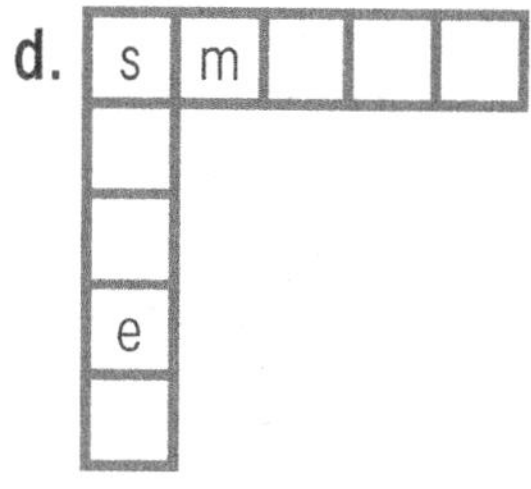

**4** Find small words inside these words. Write each small word in a sentence in your book. The first one has been done for you.

near → *ear*   *Simon had a blocked ear.*

disappear → ______   cheering → ______   speared → ______

teardrop → ______   nearby → ______   fearful → ______

**Word LIST**

beer
deer
ear
fear
jeer
gear
queer
sheer
sneer
hear
near
steer
tear
sear
year
cheer
disappear
career
shear
smear
spear
engineer
pioneer
volunteer
rear
feared
hearing
cheering
teardrop
nearby
appear
peer
clear
deer

## 5

Use the clues to unscramble these words. Write them in sentences in your book. The first one has been done for you.

| Jumbled word | Clue | New word |
|---|---|---|
| a r p s e | a weapon that you throw | **spear** – The bushman threw the spear at the cassowary. |
| a r e h s | to cut wool off a sheep | |
| a r e | you use this to hear | |
| e s t r e | you do this with a steering wheel | |
| r e b e | an alcoholic drink | |
| e d r e | an animal with antlers | |
| e r c e h | to shout for a team that is playing | |
| r a d e | very expensive | |
| u e r q e | strange | |

## 6

Choose the correct word. Write the complete sentences in your book.

a. Mum wouldn't let me buy the football because it was too (deer / dear).
b. We will (volunteer / cheer) to help at the school market.
c. The farmer will (sheer / shear) his sheep in the spring.
d. The speeding car hit our car in the (sear / rear).
e. This (fear / year) we will harvest large yams.
f. Did you (here / hear) that the policeman lived (year / near) our school?

## 7

Choose the best rhyming word. Write both words in sentences in your book.

a. cheering (feared, steering, hear, ear)
b. sneered (steered, gear, hearing, tear)
c. career (spend, care, disappear, bird)
d. year (month, day, tear, week, hour)
e. gears (hear, cheer, near, fears, fearing)

### Off the page

**What Am I?**

When you have found the answers, choose three more words of your own and write clues for them. Ask your friend to guess what the words are.

*1st letter is in **DAN** but not in **MAN**.*
*2nd letter is in **LET** but not in **LIT**.*
*3rd letter is in **MEET** but not in **MEAT**.*
*4th letter is in **RAM** but not in **DAM**.*
*What word am I?*

*1st letter is in **FUN** but not in **RUN**.*
*2nd letter is in **SET** but not in **SIT**.*
*3rd letter is in **FAN** but not in **FIN**.*
*4th letter is in **RUST** but not in **MUST**.*
*What word am I?*

*1st letter is in **YAM** but not in **SAM**.*
*2nd letter is in **SEND** but not in **SAND**.*
*3rd letter is in **TAN** but not in **TIN**.*
*4th letter is in **RUN** but not in **SUN**.*
*What word am I?*

*1st letter is in **JUG** but not in **PUG**.*
*2nd letter is in **FEND** but not in **FIND**.*
*3rd letter is in **BEND** but not in **BAND**.*
*4th letter is in **CAR** but not in **CAT**.*
*What word am I?*

# WORD KNOWLEDGE > Present tense verbs

**RULE**

Remember! **Verbs** are **action** words. If an action is happening **now**, you use the **present tense** of the verb. Many present tense verbs end in '**–ing**', for example: I like ***jogging*** in the park.

**1** Choose '–ing' verbs from the Verb Box to fill the gaps. Write the complete sentences in your book.

a. The acrobats are ______________ on the trapeze.
b. The seal is ______________ the ball.
c. The lion tamer is ______________ the whip.
d. The tiger is ______________ through the hoop.
e. The bear is ______________ the car around the ring.
f. The ringmaster is ______________ him.
g. The magician is ______________ the man in half.
h. The man in the hat is ______________ out of the cannon!

**Verb BOX**

driving
jumping
shooting
cracking
cutting
swinging
balancing
watching

**2** Write these words in sentences in your book.

clapping cheering laughing

## COMMON WORDS >

**1** Choose words from the Spelling List to fill the gaps. Write the complete sentences in your book.

a. We went to visit our ____________ yesterday.
b. My dad says that a ____________ lives at the bottom of our garden.
c. The ____________ I like best are netball and softball.
d. I like ____________ because we can stay up late.
e. My friend ____________ at our house last night.

**2** Write all the words in the Spelling List in alphabetical order

**3** Write two sentences to show different meanings for the word '**tear**'.

**Weekly Spelling List to be tested at the end of the week**

**Spelling LIST**

fairy
cousin
stayed
Friday
games
tear
career
year
cheering
steered

**Writing activity > At the Circus**

- What happens at a circus? Describe what kind of circus performer you would like to be – an acrobat, a lion tamer, a trapeze artist, a juggler, a clown? Explain why you would like to be one of these.

# FOCUS › 'y' sound (as in 'happy' / 'honey')

**1** Choose the letters '**y**' or '**ey**' to fill the gaps in these words from the Word List. Write the words in your book.

| | | | |
|---|---|---|---|
| bab__ | happ__ | pupp__ | part__ |
| hon__ __ | vall__ __ | monk __ __ | hungr__ |
| carr__ | prett __ | lad __ | all __ __ |

**2** Choose a word from the Word Bank to complete these sentences.

**Word BANK**

parsley pretty honey very party chimney hurry jockey

a. The beehive contained a lot of __ __ __ __ __.
b. The floor was __ __ __ __ dirty.
c. She wore a __ __ __ __ __ __ dress to the __ __ __ __ __.
d. Smoke was coming out of the __ __ __ __ __ __ __.
e. We grow __ __ __ __ __ __ __ in our garden.
f. We need to __ __ __ __ __ so that we are not late for school.
g. The __ __ __ __ __ __ fell off his horse.

**3** Find words from the Word List to complete these word grids. Write each pair of words in your book.

a. across: m _ n _ _ _; down: m _ n _
b. down: p a _ _ _; across: a _ _ _ _
c. across: d _ _ _ _ _; down: d _ r _ _
d. across: b _ b _; down: b _ _ _
e. across: t _ _ _; down: t r _ _ _ _ _
f. across: m _ _ _; down: m _ n _ _
g. across: t _ _ l _ _ _; down: t w _ n _ _
h. across: f _ _ n _; down: f _ r _ _

**Word LIST**

happy
many
honey
baby
donkey
body
easy
lady
monkey
journey
party
valley
ready
very
trolley
pretty
funny
turkey
jockey
carry
puppy
windy
parsley
cheeky
twenty
chimney
dirty
pony
alley
storey
tiny
angry
hungry
forty
money
hurry

**4** Find small words inside these words. Write each small word in a sentence in your book. The first one has been done for you.

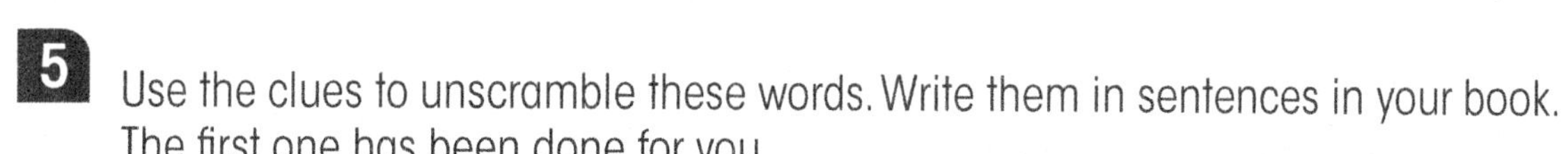

forty → for The boy asked for his breakfast.

tiny → ______ chimney → ______ twenty → ______ funny → ______

ready → ______ party → ______ many → ______ storey → ______

**5** Use the clues to unscramble these words. Write them in sentences in your book. The first one has been done for you.

| Jumbled word | Clue | New word |
| --- | --- | --- |
| r e t t p y | beautiful | pretty – The actress was very pretty. |
| n y o p | a small horse | |
| u r y r h | to move quickly | |
| k r e u t y | a large farmyard bird | |
| k y e j c o | someone who rides racehorses | |
| r y a n g | very cross | |
| w t t y e n | a number one less than 21 | |
| e m y o n k | a small animal that climbs trees | |
| u p y p p | a young dog | |

**6** Choose the correct word. Write the complete sentences in your book.

a. The (baby / body) was (very / merry) small.
b. The (donkey / trolley) was found in the bush eating grass.
c. The (angry / hungry) dog went looking for food.
d. The (cheeky / dirty) bird flew down and stole the dog's food.
e. The (jockey / journey) to Madang took a long time.
f. We needed (monkey / money) to buy an ice-cream cone at the store.

## Off the page

**What Am I?**

When you have found the answers, choose three more words of your own and write clues for them. Ask your friend to guess what the words are.

*I have six letters.*
*I begin with the letter 't' and end with the letter 'y'.*
*I am a bird that can't fly.*
*I am a ______.*

*I have seven letters.*
*Two of my letters are vowels.*
*I am used in a supermarket.*
*I am a ______.*

*I have six letters.*
*Two of my letters are vowels.*
*The two vowels are the same.*
*I am ______.*

*I have five letters.*
*Three of my letters are 'p'.*
*I am a baby animal.*
*I am a ______.*

# WORD KNOWLEDGE > Adverbs

**RULE**

**Adverbs** tell us more about the verb. They tell us **how** something is done.
They often end in '**–ly**', for example: *Colitha ran quickly*.
The adverb '*quickly*' tells us how Colitha ran.

**1** Copy these sentences into your book. Underline the adverbs.

a. Joseph cried loudly when the bee stung him.
b. Mum whispered quietly in the baby's ear.
c. The old woman walked slowly down the stairs.
d. The lion roared angrily at his keeper.

**2** Write sentences in your book with these adverbs.

slowly gently bravely brightly

**3** Choose the best adverb to complete each sentence.
Write the complete sentences in your book.

a. Dad held the baby kitten (gently / tightly).
b. Grandpa snored (loudly / sweetly).
c. The horse galloped (greedily / quickly) along the track.
d. The boy played (quietly / swiftly) in his room.
e. The teacher spoke (hungrily / clearly) to the class.

# COMMON WORDS >

**1** Choose words from the Spelling List to fill the gaps.
Write the complete sentences in your book.

a. I _ _ _ _ up at seven o'clock this morning.
b. Can you _ _ _ _ to my house to play?
c. The teacher said, "If you are _ _ _ _ late again you will be in trouble!"
d. Joseph kicked the _ _ _ _ over the fence.
e. The _ _ _ man had to use a walking stick.

**2** Complete the counting pattern up to one hundred.

ten ______ thirty ______ ______ sixty ______ eighty ______ one hundred

Weekly Spelling List to be tested at the end of the week

**Spelling LIST**

old
woke
ball
come
ever
happy
honey
twenty
easy
journey

**Writing activity > How Lucky Are You?**

- Are you lucky or unlucky?
Write about times when you have been very lucky or very unlucky, or both!

# FOCUS > 'or' sound (as in 'saw' / 'fort')

**Word LIST**

paw, saw, for, corn, dawn, lawn, horn, born, crawl, shawl, torn, jaw, crawled, fawn, brawl, worn, scorn, sworn, pawn, prawn, yawn, fork, stork, form, font, law, raw, caw, port, draw, claw, morning, storm, north, straw, strawberry, pawpaw, seesaw, horse, report, pork, cork, storming, short, force

**1** Choose the letters '**aw**' or '**or**' to fill the gaps in these words from the Word List. Write the words in your book.

| | | | |
|---|---|---|---|
| s__ __ | sh__ __l | f__ __m | c__ __n |
| rep__ __t | cr__ __l | p__ __ | h__ __se |
| y__ __n | h__ __n | l__ __ | n__ __th |

**2** Choose a word from the Word Bank to complete these sentences.

**Word BANK**

morning brawl north pawpaw hawk torch dawn draw

a. We had to travel __ __ __ __ __ to reach the village.
b. The __ __ __ __ __ __ was very juicy and sweet.
c. There was a __ __ __ __ __ outside the courtroom.
d. The __ __ __ __ circled in the sky trying to catch a chicken.
e. The night was dark so we used a __ __ __ __ __ to get home.
f. The sun rises at __ __ __ __.
g. I like to __ __ __ __ pictures in my book.
h. My mother goes to the store every __ __ __ __ __ __ __.

**3** Find words from the Word List to complete these word grids.
Choose one word from each grid and write it in a sentence in your book.

a.
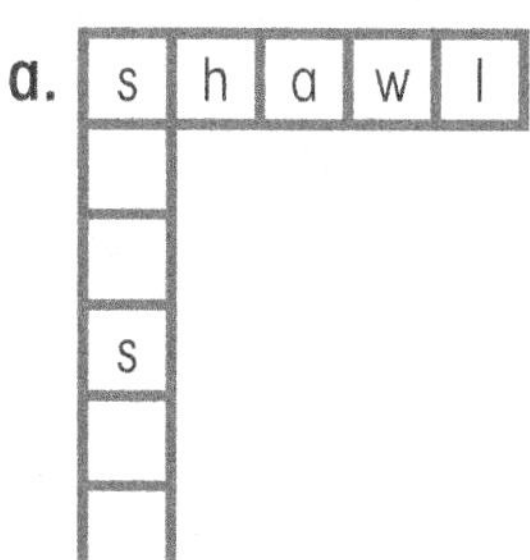

b.

c.
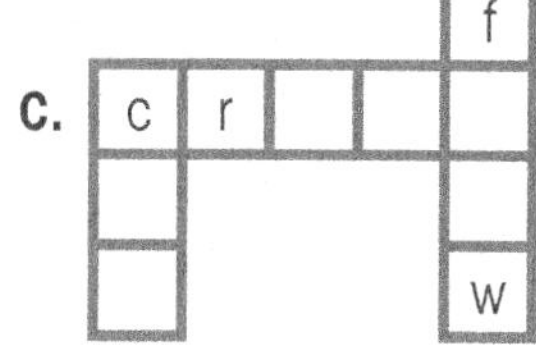

d.
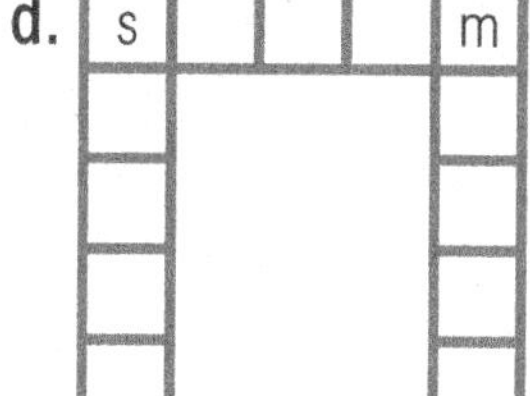
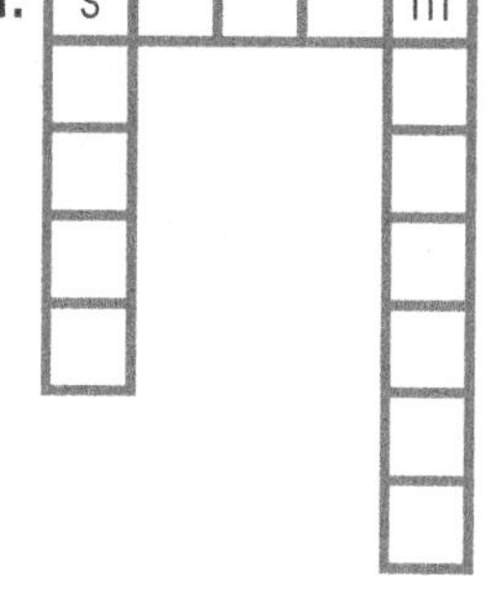

e.
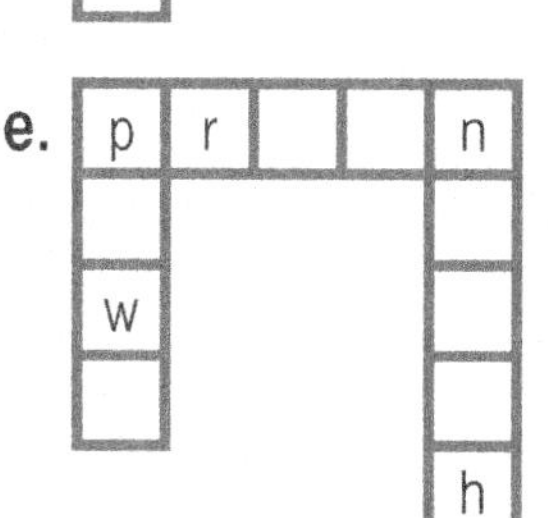

f.
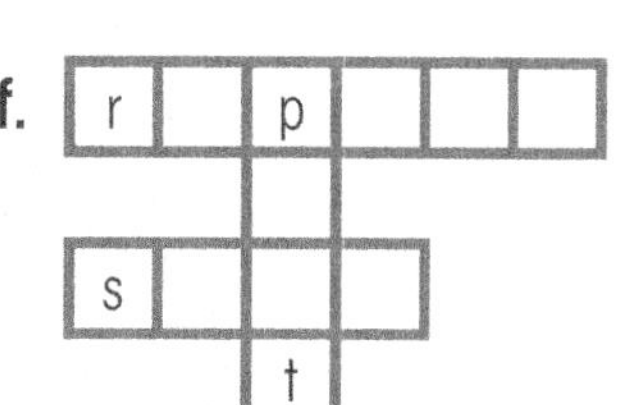

g.
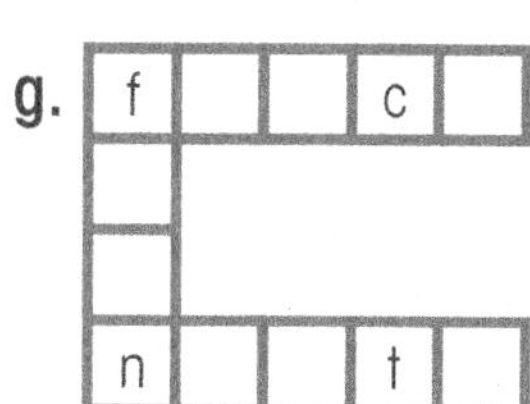

## 4

Use the clues to unscramble these words. Write them in sentences in your book. The first one has been done for you.

| Jumbled word | Clue | New word |
|---|---|---|
| t o r f | army building | **fort** – The fort had very high walls. |
| o r h t n | a direction on a compass | |
| r n o c | another word for maize | |
| r p n w a | a sea animal | |
| k f r o | an eating utensil | |
| l b r a w | a fight involving many people | |
| w a p w a p | a tropical fruit | |
| r e s h o | an animal | |
| t r e r p o | a newspaper article | |

## 5

Choose the correct word. Write the complete sentences in your book.

a. The old woman wore a (shorn / shawl) to keep warm.
b. The shoes had many holes because they were very (worn / wore).
c. It is rude to (yawn / pawn) in class.
d. The sheep have been (scorn / shorn) so that the wool can be sold at market.
e. We all had to wear (short / snort) pants for sports day.
f. The baby deer is called a (flaw / fawn).

## 6

Choose the best rhyming word. Write both words in sentences in your book.

a. storm (swore, form, torn, fork)
b. pork (law, cork, shawl, wore)
c. brawled (saw, poor, crawled, for)
d. yawn (dawn, hawk, report, morning)
e. short (fawn, caw, seesaw, snort)
f. brawl (sort, crawl, straw, paw)

### Off the page

**What Am I?**

When you have found the answers, choose three more words of your own and write clues for them. Ask your friend to guess what the words are.

*I have five letters.*
*I begin with the letter 's' and end with the letter 't'.*
*I am not long.*
*I am ________.*

*I have six letters.*
*Three of my letters are vowels.*
*I am in a playground.*
*I am a ________.*

*I have five letters.*
*I have only have one vowel.*
*Babies do this before they walk.*
*I am ________.*

*I have four letters.*
*My last letter is 'k'.*
*I am used to seal a bottle.*
*I am a ________.*

# WORD KNOWLEDGE > Adverbs

**RULE**

Remember! **Adverbs** tell more about the verb. They tell **how** something is done. They often end in '**–ly**', for example: *slowly, kindly.*

**1** Choose '–ly' adverbs from the Adverb Box to fill the gaps. Write the complete sentences in your book.

a. Pigs grunt _ _ _ _ _ _ _.
b. Cats creep _ _ _ _ _ _ _ _.
c. Cheetahs run _ _ _ _ _ _ _.
d. Turtles walk _ _ _ _ _ _.
e. Snails slide _ _ _ _ _ _ _ _.
f. Monkeys chatter _ _ _ _ _ _.

**Adverb BOX**

quickly
slowly
smoothly
silently
noisily
loudly

**2** Write sentences in your book with these adverbs.

greedily carefully strongly neatly

# COMMON WORDS >

**1** Choose words from the Spelling List to fill the gaps. Write the complete sentences in your book.

a. My brother is _ _ _ _ _ _ of mice.
b. Joseph's _ _ _ _ is always untidy.
c. Did you see _ _ _ took the book?
d. We bought a _ _ _ car yesterday.
e. I hope it will be a _ _ _ _ day for the picnic.

Weekly Spelling List to be tested at the end of the week

**2** Write the words from the Spelling List in alphabetical order in your book.

**Spelling LIST**

new
room
nice
scared
who
seesaw
pawpaw
report
cork
morning

**Writing activity > Follow the Instructions**

- Write some instructions for a friend to follow.
  For example, 'Jump three times and nod your head.'
  Don't just tell them what to do – tell them how to do it using an adverb.
  For example, 'Jump lightly three times and nod your head slowly.'
- Brainstorm some more adverbs you could use before you start.
  Swap your instructions with a friend.

Revision

# FOCUS › 'a', 'eer' sounds

**1** Copy these tables. Write words from Word Bank ① into the correct box.

Add two words of your own to the correct box.

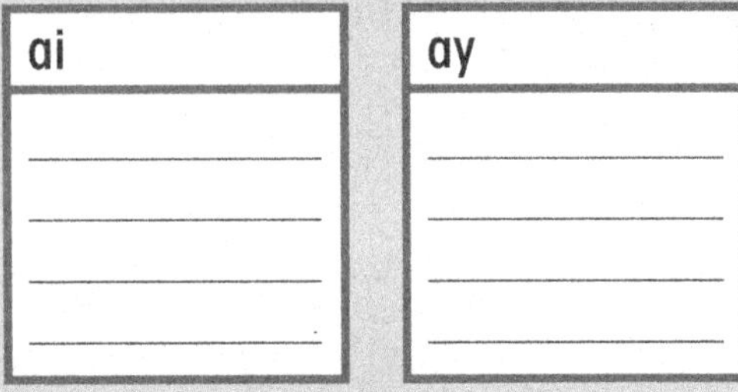

| ai | ay |
|---|---|
| | |
| | |
| | |
| | |

**2** Write the three words beginning with '**sp–**' in sentences in your book.

**3** Write each of these words in a sentence in your book to show its meaning.

bail main mane maid made mail male tail pale pail

**4** Copy these tables. Write words from Word Bank ② into the correct box.

Add two words of your own to the correct box.

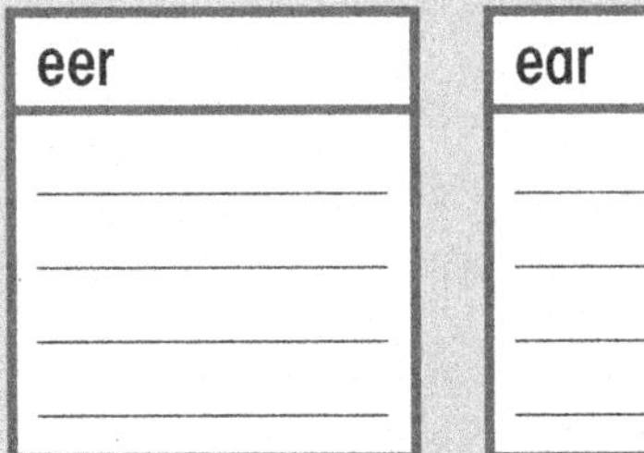

| eer | ear |
|---|---|
| | |
| | |
| | |
| | |

**5** Write the six words beginning with '**s–**' in sentences of your own.

**6** Write each of these words in a sentence in your book to show its meaning.

ear fear beer hear tear appear nearby year spear

**7** Copy these words into your book. Circle the odd one out.

| | | | | | |
|---|---|---|---|---|---|
| **a.** | steer | queer | hear | cheer | sneer |
| **b.** | fear | jeer | year | rear | near |
| **c.** | career | volunteer | pioneer | giraffe | queer |
| **d.** | hear | near | nearby | queue | tear |
| **e.** | beer | cheer | sheer | spring | deer |
| **f.** | ear | eye | gear | teardrop | spear |

**Word BANK ①**

fail
hay
paint
rain
day
faint
bay
tray
pain
lay
tail
laid
sway
sprain
brain
may
rail
spray
jail
day
stay
chain
Spain

**Word BANK ②**

steer
ear
fear
queer
sneer
gear
appear
jeer
shear
hear
near
tear
career
pioneer
nearby
year
beer
deer
sheer
cheer
rear
smear
voluntee
eardrop
spear

# FOCUS > 'y', 'or' sounds

**1** Copy these tables. Write words from Word Bank ③ into the correct box.

Add two words of your own to the correct box.

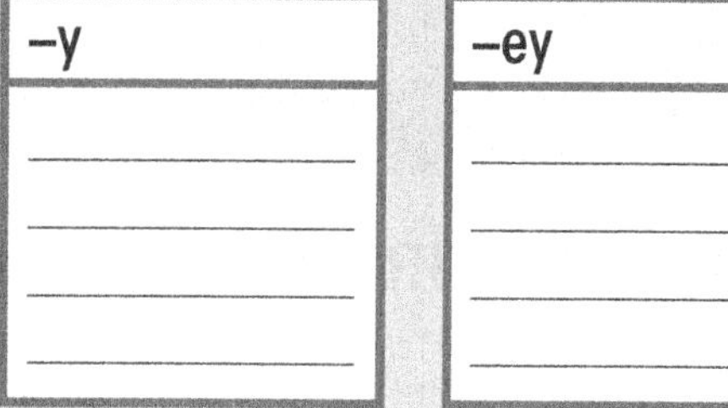

| –y | –ey |
| --- | --- |
| | |

**2** Write the three words beginning with '**every–**' in sentences in your book.

**3** Write each of these words in a sentence in your book to show its meaning.

turkey hungry chimney monkey puppy pretty journey valley

**4** Find three compound words beginning with the word '**every**'. Write them in sentences in your book.

**5** Copy these tables. Write words from Word Bank ④ into the correct box.

Add two words of your own to the correct box.

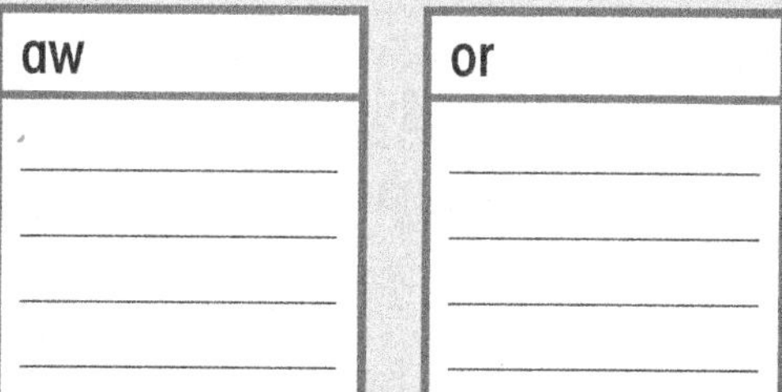

| aw | or |
| --- | --- |
| | |

**6** Write the three words beginning with '**st–**' in sentences in your book.

**7** Write each of these words in a sentence in your book to show its meaning.

crawl worn pawpaw fork seesaw jaw torn north

**8** Copy these words into your book. Circle the odd one out.

| | | | | | |
| --- | --- | --- | --- | --- | --- |
| a. | turkey | plenty | donkey | monkey | valley |
| b. | funny | pretty | ready | hungry | alley |
| c. | twenty | ten | fifty | sixty | forty |
| d. | very | lady | nearly | nearby | ready |

**9** There are three words beginning with '**p–**' in Word Bank ④. Write them in your book in alphabetical order.

## Word BANK ③

turkey, very, pretty, easy, plenty, baby, donkey, party, valley, ready, funny, jockey, parsley, alley, hungry, forty, chimney, lady, journey, ready, trolley, puppy, pony, tiny, everything, everyone, everywhere

## Word BANK ④

saw, for, corn, lawn, born, shawl, crawl, torn, jaw, crawled, worn, prawn, strawberry, fork, scorn, form, storming, law, port, sworn, sort, claw, north, cork, pawpaw, seesaw, storm

## FOCUS › 'ow' sound (as in 'sound' / 'cow')

**Word LIST**

| | |
|---|---|
| sound | wow |
| found | pound |
| cow | sound |
| how | account |
| count | amount |
| mount | scout |
| now | spout |
| prowl | allow |
| shout | eyebrow |
| row | pouch |
| cloud | background |
| sow | discount |
| couch | lout |
| ground | aloud |
| mount | loud |
| proud | somehow |
| crouch | anyhow |
| vow | round |
| bound | hound |

**1** Choose the letters '**ou**' or '**ow**' to fill the gaps in these words from the Word List. Write the words in your book.

| | | | |
|---|---|---|---|
| gr__ __nd | s__ __ | r__ __nd | n__ __ |
| sp__ __t | am __ __nt | all__ __ | l__ __d |
| p__ __ch | c__ __nt | c__ __ | w__ __ |

**2** Choose a word from the Word Bank to complete these sentences.

**Word BANK**

row allow account ground shout how discount crouch

a. Our school opened an __ __ __ __ __ __ __ at South Pacific Bank.
b. I wonder __ __ __ we will cross this flowing creek.
c. The boys had a __ __ __ at the back of the school grounds.
d. The tiger will __ __ __ __ __ __ very low to catch his prey.
e. The baby boy fell to the __ __ __ __ __ __ and hurt his knee.
f. Mum will not __ __ __ __ __ me to stay up late on school nights.
g. The policeman had to __ __ __ __ __ very loudly to get the crowd's attention.
h. Mum gets a __ __ __ __ __ __ __ __ at the store because she buys a lot of things.

**3** Use this code breaker to find the missing words.
Write the words in your book in complete sentences.

| a | b | c | d | e | f | g | h | i | j | k | l | m | n | o | p | q | r | s | t | u | v | w | x | y | z |
|---|---|---|---|---|---|---|---|---|---|---|---|---|---|---|---|---|---|---|---|---|---|---|---|---|---|
| 26 | 25 | 24 | 23 | 22 | 21 | 20 | 19 | 18 | 17 | 16 | 15 | 14 | 13 | 12 | 11 | 10 | 9 | 8 | 7 | 6 | 5 | 4 | 3 | 2 | 1 |

a. (24, 12, 6, 13, 7) b. (8, 11, 12, 6, 7) c. (8, 12, 14, 22, 19, 12, 4)
d. (4, 12, 6, 13, 23) e. (26, 15, 15, 12, 4) f. (22, 2, 22, 25, 9, 12, 4)

**4** Find small words inside these words. Write each small word in a sentence in your book.
The first one has been done for you.

discount → *count* *The shopkeeper said he would count up what we owed him.*

amount → ______ cloud → ______ background → ______
somehow → ______ ground → ______ anyhow → ______

**5** Find words from the Word List that have a similar meaning to these words. Write the words in sentences in your book. The first one has been done for you.

female pig → *sow* *The sow looks after her piglets.*

to call loudly →

an animal that produces milk →

a type of dog →

noises →

this produces rain →

to stalk →

a small container →

tied up →

**6** Choose the correct word. Write the words in complete sentences in your book.

**a.** The old woman tripped and fell to the (hound / ground).
**b.** We will finish our work (how / now).
**c.** My dad has a bank (amount / account).
**d.** The animal (crouched / pouched) low in the tall grass.
**e.** The lost dog will find his way home (eyebrow / somehow).
**f.** We bought a new (vouch / couch) for our living room.

**7** Use the clues to find the words in these puzzles. Write them in your book. The first one has been done for you.

**a.** e y e b r o w (across); b o u n d (down)
**Across:** sits above the eye
**Down:** tied up

**b.** g r _ _ _ _ _ (across); g r _ _ _ (down)
**Across:** an angry person
**Down:** an angry sound

**c.** _ h _ _ _ (across); h _ _ (down)
**Across:** to yell
**Down:** a question word

**d.** c _ _ (across); c _ _ _ _ h (down)
**Across:** an animal that gives milk
**Down:** a comfortable seat for more than one person to sit on

**e.** a c c _ _ _ _ (across); a _ _ _ _ (down)
**Across:** a way to keep money in a bank
**Down:** to let or permit

**f.** c _ _ _ _ (across); c l _ _ _ _ (down)
**Across:** to say numbers in order
**Down:** they float in the sky

**RHYME time** › Copy this rhyme into your book and then ...

1. Circle all the '**–out**' words.
2. Make up your own rhymes using '**ow**' words.

*Girls yell,*
*Boys shout,*
*Dogs bark,*
*School's out!*

*In and out,*
*Thin and stout,*
*Pig's snout,*
*You're out!*

# WORD KNOWLEDGE > Pronouns

**RULE**

A **pronoun** is a word that is used in place of a noun, for example: *he, she, it.*
The boy kicked three goals – 'boy' is a noun. He kicked three goals – 'He' is a pronoun.

**1** Choose pronouns from the Pronoun Box to fill the gaps.
Write the complete sentences in your book.

a. Jason walked into the classroom and __ __ hit the boy.
b. Lela cut her finger and __ __ __ began to cry.
c. The children began talking and then __ __ __ __ began shouting.
d. The man picked up __ __ __ hammer and hit the nail.
e. The snail crawled up the stalk and then __ __ ate the leaf.

**Pronoun BOX**

| | |
|---|---|
| I | it |
| we | they |
| you | his |
| he | her |
| she | |

**2** Rewrite these sentences in your book and underline the pronouns.

a. She went with her brother.
b. I want to see it before you go.
c. Did you go to her home?
d. Did they know it was his pencil?
e. The teacher asked if we could be quiet.

**3** Write these pronouns in sentences in your book. you we they

# COMMON WORDS >

**1** Choose words from the Spelling List to fill the gaps.
Write the complete sentences in your book.

a. It was raining so we had to come __ __ __ __ __ __.
b. I like chocolate __ __ __ __ the best.
c. The teacher said my painting was the __ __ __ __ in the class.
d. The possum climbed up the __ __ __ __.
e. Come and see if __ __ __ __ still in the tree.

**Spelling LIST**

inside
it's
tree
cake
best
sound
count
loud
allow
prowl

**2** The word 'sound' ends in '**–ound**'.
Write five more words in your book that end in '**–ound**'.

**Writing activity > Favourite Foods**

- What is your favourite meal to eat? Write about how you make it.
Don't forget to list the ingredients and then list the instructions with the steps to follow.

# Unit 22

## FOCUS > 'oy' sound (as in 'boy' / 'coin')

**Word LIST**

boy, joy, coin, join, coy, groin, ploy, loin, rejoin, toy, ahoy, annoy, joint, point, convoy, cowboy, appoint, hoist, moist, decoy, destroy, boil, oil, coil, employ, foil, soil, enjoy, spoil, toil, schoolboy, void, avoid, choice, tomboy, sirloin

**1** Choose the letters '**oi**' or '**oy**' to fill the gaps in these words from the Word List. Write the words in your book.

| | | | |
|---|---|---|---|
| pl___ | j___nt | b___l | l___n |
| sp___l | dec___ | av___d | p___nt |
| j___n | enj___ | t___ | j___ |

**2** Choose a word from the Word Bank to complete these sentences.

**Word BANK**

joy annoy toil avoid appoint boil alloy groin

a. We need to __________ crossing the river when it is flowing very fast.
b. We were full of ______ when we heard the good news.
c. The headmaster will ______________ a new teacher for our grade.
d. We need to ________ the water from the creek before we drink it.
e. Steel is made by joining one __________ together with another.
f. The pesky bird continued to __________ the farmer.
g. The villagers will ________ long and hard to harvest the crop.
h. The athlete injured his __________ during the race.

**3** Use this code breaker to find the missing words.
Write the words in your book in complete sentences.

| a | b | c | d | e | f | g | h | i | j | k | l | m | n | o | p | q | r | s | t | u | v | w | x | y | z |
|---|---|---|---|---|---|---|---|---|---|---|---|---|---|---|---|---|---|---|---|---|---|---|---|---|---|
| 26 | 25 | 24 | 23 | 22 | 21 | 20 | 19 | 18 | 17 | 16 | 15 | 14 | 13 | 12 | 11 | 10 | 9 | 8 | 7 | 6 | 5 | 4 | 3 | 2 | 1 |

a. (26, 5, 12, 18, 23) b. (23, 22, 24, 12, 2) c. (8, 18, 9, 15, 12, 18, 13)
d. (15, 12, 18, 13) e. (24, 12, 13, 5, 12, 2) f. (22, 14, 11, 15, 12, 2)

**4** Find small words inside these words. Write each small word in a sentence in your book.
The first one has been done for you.

appoint → *point* *You should not point your finger at someone.*

tomboy → ______ spoiled → ______ enjoy → ______
rejoin → ______ soil → ______ hoisted → ______

## 5 Find words from the Word List that have a similar meaning to these words. Write the words in sentences in your book. The first one has been done for you.

to heat liquid → *boil* *We boil the water to make tea.*

to twist → ______ to ruin → ______ dirt → ______

type of meat → ______ a trap → ______ metal money → ______

to irritate → ______ the opposite of girl → ______

## 6 Choose the correct word. Write the words in complete sentences in your book.

a. The director will (anoint / appoint) a new store manager.
b. The heavy rain will (decoy / destroy) the banana crop.
c. The (cowboy / convoy) of trucks drove slowly up the mountain.
d. The sailor yelled out (alloy / ahoy) as his ship came into port.
e. The builder will (hoist / moist) the timber beams to the top of the building
f. The sick boy will (rejoin / joint) his classmates at camp when he gets better.
g. The manager will (employ / enjoy) ten more people.
h. The (cowboy / toy) rode across the mountain.

## 7 Use the clues to find the words in these puzzles. Write them in your book. The first one has been done for you.

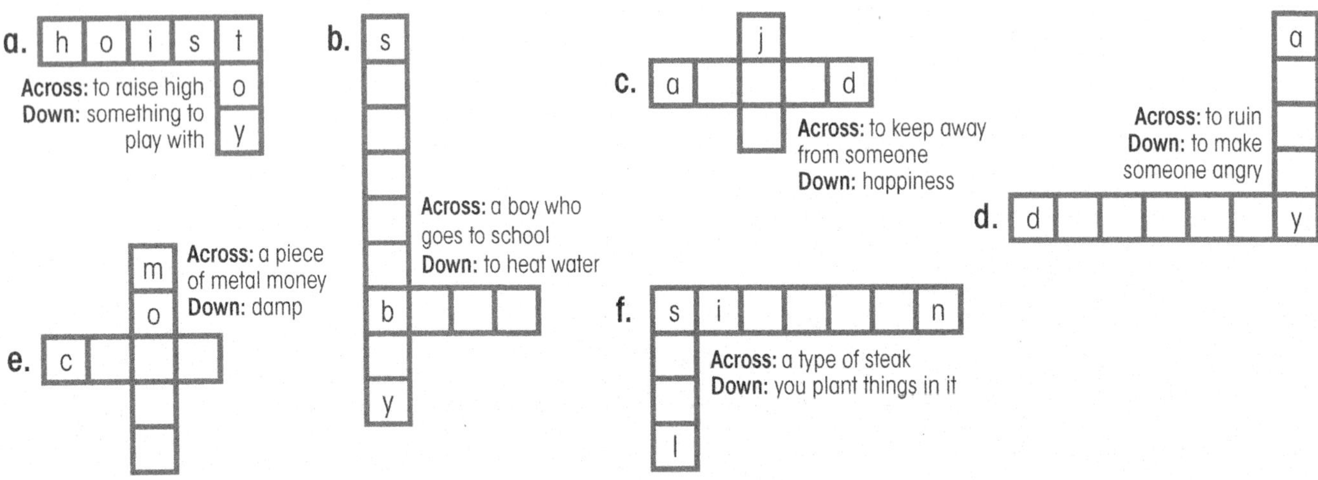

**RHYME time ›** Copy this rhyme into your book and then ...

1. Circle the '**–oil**' words.
2. Write the '**–oil**' words in sentences.

*Mary had a little lamb she fed it castor oil.*
*And everywhere the lamb would go it fertilised the soil!*

# WORD KNOWLEDGE > Sentences

**RULE**

A **sentence** is a group of words that always has a **verb**.
It begins with a capital letter and ends with a full stop, a question mark or an exclamation mark.
A sentence should always make sense.

**1** Complete these sentences with verbs from the Verb Box.

a. The dogs _ _ _ _ _ _ very loudly.
b. We _ _ _ spaghetti for dinner.
c. Please _ _ _ _ the light off.
d. I _ _ _ _ my bike to school.
e. We _ _ _ _ _ _ basketball at lunchtime.
f. I will _ _ _ _ _ a fish for dinner.

**Verb BOX**

- turn
- catch
- barked
- played
- rode
- ate

**2** Complete these sentences with your own words. Write them in your book.
Remember that sentences should always make sense.

a. Most cats ______.
b. I like to ______.
c. The speeding car ______.
d. The angry lion ______.
e. Puppies and kittens ______.

# COMMON WORDS >

**1** Choose words from the Spelling List to fill the gaps.
Write the complete sentences in your book.

a. The horse had a very _ _ _ _ tail.
b. The baby bird _ _ _ _ out of the nest.
c. I don't know _ _ _ to fix the broken gate.
d. On Friday nights we can watch a _ _ _ _ _ on TV.
e. Kick the _ _ _ _ _ _ ball into the net.

**2** Write the compound word from the Spelling List in your book.

**3** Write the smaller words in the compound word in sentences in your book.

**Spelling LIST**

- fell
- long
- movie
- soccer
- how
- choice
- annoy
- join
- cowboy
- spoil

**Writing activity > What Pet is Best?**

- What kind of pet is best? Write your opinion about what kind of animal would make the best pet. Make sure all your sentences make sense.

# Unit 23

## FOCUS › 'air' sound (as in 'chair' / 'bare')

**1** Choose the letters '**air**' or '**are**' to fill the gaps in these words from the Word List. Write the words in your book.

| | | | |
|---|---|---|---|
| bl__ __ __ | __ __ __ | fl__ __ __ | ch__ __ __ |
| h__ __ __ | rep__ __ __ | sp__ __ __ | unf__ __ __ |
| squ__ __ __ | st__ __ __ | p__ __ __ | d__ __ __ |

**2** Choose a word from the Word Bank to complete these sentences.

**Word BANK**

aware armchair mare spare funfair hardware lair beware

a. Grandpa likes to sit in his ______.
b. The ______ came first in the horse race.
c. The sign said: '______ of the dog'.
d. Do you have a ______ pencil to lend me?
e. We would love to go to the ______.
f. We will buy the nails in the ______ store.
g. He was ______ that the dog was following him.
h. The fox had a ______ close to our village.

**✱ RULE**

Remember, a **homophone** is a word with the same sound as another word, but with different spelling and a different meaning, for example: *fare* and *fair*.

**3** Read these words and write each one in your book with its meaning. The first pair is done for you.

hare → *a large rabbit*
hair → *the covering on your head*
flare →
flair →
stare →
stair →
fair →
fare →

**Word LIST**

| | |
|---|---|
| air | pair |
| bare | repair |
| airport | stair |
| airway | snare |
| blare | spare |
| care | square |
| chair | stairway |
| dare | armchair |
| chairman | stare |
| chairlift | aware |
| glare | beware |
| hare | funfair |
| mare | unfair |
| fair | wheelchc |
| flair | beware |
| hair | hardware |
| rare | dairy |
| lair | nightmar |
| scare | prepare |
| share | fairy |
| flare | pare |

**4** Use the beginning sounds to write '**–air**' and '**–are**' words.
You might need to add extra letters to complete the words.

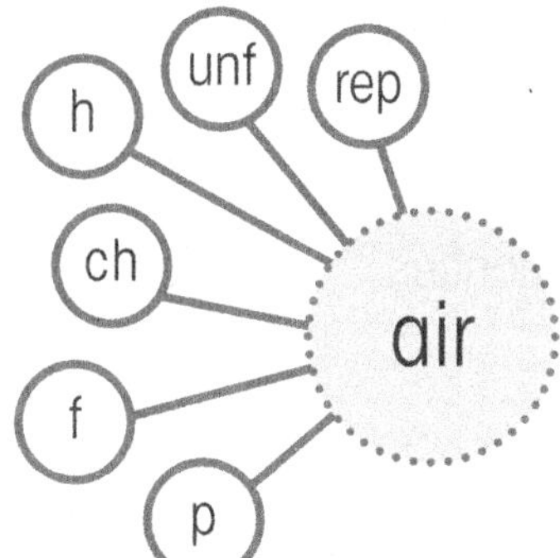


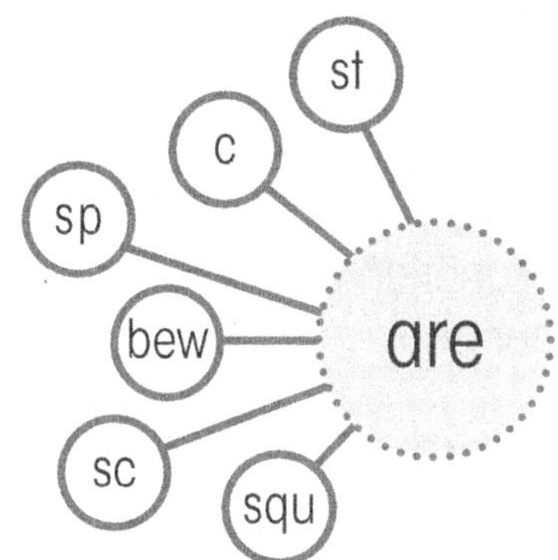


**5** Find words from the Word List that have a similar meaning to these words.
Write the words in sentences in your book. The first one has been done for you.

the covering on our head → *hair* *Grandma has grey hair.*

| | |
|---|---|
| to look very closely → | to frighten → |
| a set of two → | we breathe this → |
| to make a loud noise → | to divide equally → |
| a bad dream → | where a plane lands → |

**6** Choose the correct word. Write the words in complete sentences in your book.

**a.** She wore her (hare / hair) in a ponytail.
**b.** He bought a (pair / pear) of shoes at the market.
**c.** Don't (stair / stare) at the old man walking down the street.
**d.** He paid his (fair / fare) on the PMV bus.
**e.** Mum will (prepare / repair) dinner when we get home.
**f.** Don't you (dare / dear) hit that little boy!

Find words from the Word List in this word search puzzle. Write them in your book.

| | | | | | | | | | | | | |
|---|---|---|---|---|---|---|---|---|---|---|---|---|
| m | b | d | f | h | j | i | g | e | c | a | q | l |
| o | n | v | i | s | q | u | a | r | e | b | m | a |
| p | x | o | n | a | z | r | i | d | c | n | d | i |
| s | n | a | r | e | p | y | r | v | o | c | g | r |
| h | i | j | k | m | z | q | p | x | y | u | x | w |
| a | v | u | t | s | q | p | o | r | w | n | p | u |
| r | a | r | e | r | f | a | r | e | s | h | v | z |
| e | x | w | s | y | a | e | t | z | c | a | r | e |
| v | u | t | g | f | i | n | k | j | l | i | u | t |
| a | y | x | d | u | r | v | e | w | c | r | b | z |

**RHYME time** › Copy this rhyme into your book and then ...

1. Underline all the '**–are**' words.
2. Circle all the '**air**' words.
3. Write two sentences in your book to show the different meanings of '**bare**' and '**bear**'.

*Don't stop and stare*
*or glare at the hairy bear,*
*Because he is bare!*

*Hairy bears do not wear*
*any clothes,*
*They just don't care!*

# WORD KNOWLEDGE > Conjunctions

**RULE**

A **conjunction** is a joining word, for example: *and, but, or, yet, because, as, if, both, before, since, like, for.* Maria went to the market and Pia went to the market. The conjunction is 'and'.

**1** Choose a conjunction from the Conjunction Box to complete these sentences. Write the complete sentences in your book.

a. The fire would not light ___________ the wood was wet.
b. They walked a long way _____ there was still a long way to go.
c. John went to the park _____ his mum and dad went too.
d. The water was too cold ___ I did not go for a swim.
e. Lela's hair was very dirty __________ she washed it.
f. Grandpa was very tired ___ he went to bed.

**Conjunction Box**

so
but
and
before
because

**2** Write sentences in your book with these conjunctions.

or but because before and

## COMMON WORDS >

**1** Choose words from the Spelling List to fill the gaps. Write the complete sentences in your book.

a. Simon ran ______ in the race.
b. I was so excited that I could not get to ________ last night.
c. You must bring your coat and ______ your hat.
d. We could see the fish _____________ in the pond.
e. The teacher wanted to ______ who called out.

**2** Write two words from the Spelling List that have the letters '**are**' in your book.

**3** Write three words from the Spelling List that have the letters '**air**' in your book.

Weekly Spelling List to be tested at the end of the week

**Spelling LIST**

also
know
last
sleep
swimming
air
chair
bare
square
dairy

**Writing activity > Who Do You Know?**

- Write a description of someone you know. Describe how they look, what they wear and what they like to do. Check to see how many conjunctions you used. Circle them.

Unit 24

# FOCUS > 'ar' sound (as in 'path' / 'car' / 'half')

**Word LIST**

calf, half, car, jar, bath, path, dark, shark, spark, mask, flask, darn, harm, farm, far, class, pass, fast, mark, star, smart, dart, glass, basketball, basket, passport, star, art, starfish, father, banana, part, party, calm, palm, tomato, part, plaster, ask, ark, arm, park, halves

**1** Choose the letters 'a', 'al' or 'ar' to fill the gaps in these words from the Word List. Write the words in your book.

| | | | |
|---|---|---|---|
| b__th | c__ __m | gl__ss | p__ss |
| pl__ster | p__ __ty | b__n__n__ | cl__ss |
| sh__ __k | c__ __ | sm__ __t | |

**2** Choose a word from the Word Bank to complete these sentences.

tomato father starfish plaster bath mask palm harm

a. We saw a s__ __ __ __ __ __ __ __ in the water.
b. Dad will p__ __ __ __ __ __ __ the walls of my room tomorrow.
c. My mum will plant t__ __ __ __ __ __ plants in our garden.
d. The air was so bad that I needed to wear a m__ __ __.
e. We saw large p__ __ __ trees growing along the beach.
f. The robber didn't h__ __ __ the young girl.
g. The dirty dog needed a b__ __ __.
h. My f__ __ __ __ __ will pick me up from school in his car.

**3** Find words from the Word List that have a similar meaning to these words. Write the words in sentences in your book. The first one has been done for you.

a woven container → *basket* *Mum bought a new basket at the market.*

| | | |
|---|---|---|
| very quick → ______ | a red plant food → ______ | two equal parts → ______ |
| very clever → ______ | a grade → ______ | a young cow → ______ |
| a vehicle → ______ | a dad → ______ | |

**4** Find small words inside these words. Write each small word in a sentence in your book. The first one has been done for you.

harm → *arm* *Joseph broke his arm when he fell.*

| | | | |
|---|---|---|---|
| start → ______ | flask → ______ | shark → ______ | basketball → ______ |
| passport → ______ | starfish → ______ | party → ______ | spark → ______ |

## 5 Choose the correct word. Write the words in complete sentences in your book.

a. The boy went right (pass / past) the school.
b. The sea was very (palm / calm) yesterday.
c. The man broke the (class / glass) bottle on the (path / bath).
d. I had a (mask / flask) of coffee in my bag.
e. Joe went for a walk in the (part / park).
f. The baby (half / calf) was sucking milk from his mother.

## 6 Find words from the Word List to complete these word grids.
Choose one word from each grid and write it in a sentence in your book.

a.
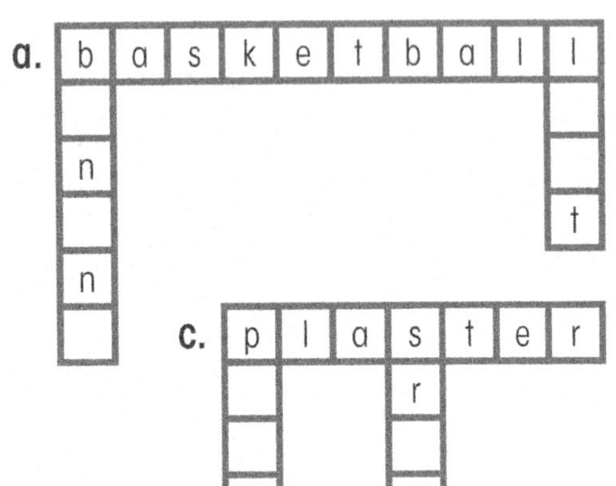


b.
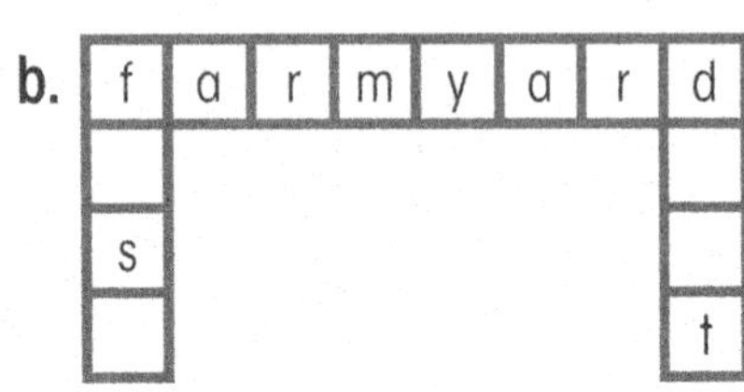


c. p l a s t e r
r
h
t

d.
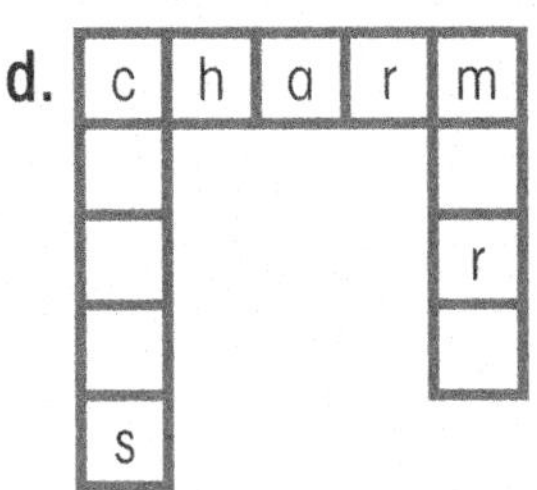


## 7 Choose the best rhyming word. Write both words in sentences in your book.

a. car (bask, plaster, far, calm)
b. art (calf, path, pass, part)
c. park (party, ask, tomato, spark)
d. calm (father, palm, basket, darn)
e. father (mark, rather, star, harm)
f. glass (basket, pass, farm, tart)

### Off the page

**What Am I?**
When you have found the answers, choose three more words of your own and write clues for them. Ask your friend to guess what the words are.

*I have eight letters.*
*I live in the sea.*
*I am shaped like a star.*
*I am a ________.*

*I have six letters.*
*I am red.*
*I grow on a vine.*
*I am a ________.*

*I have five letters.*
*You drink from me.*
*I don't have handles.*
*I am a ________.*

*I have four letters.*
*I drink milk.*
*I am a baby cow.*
*I am a ________.*

*I have four letters.*
*I am in the sky.*
*I twinkle.*
*I am a ________.*

*I have five letters.*
*I live in the sea.*
*I have large, sharp teeth.*
*I am a ________.*

# WORD KNOWLEDGE › Prepositions

**RULE**

A **preposition** tells where or when something is.
A preposition goes in front of a noun or pronoun to show **place**, **position** or **time**, for example: *in, on, under, around, with.*
The cat is *under* the bed. The preposition is '*under*'.
The dog is *on* the mat. The preposition is '*on*'.

**1** Choose a preposition from the Preposition Box to complete each sentence. Write the complete sentences in your book.

a. The hat is _ _ the old man's head.
b. The bird flew _ _ the chimney.
c. The taxi drove _ _ _ _ _ the road.
d. The toddler stood _ _ _ _ _ _ _ the pram.
e. Humpty Dumpty fell _ _ _ _ the wall.

**2** Find words from the Preposition Box in this word search puzzle. Write them in your book.

| u | n | d | e | r |
|---|---|---|---|---|
| f | g | o | b | e |
| o | n | w | y | v |
| t | i | n | t | o |
| w | o | l | e | b |

**Preposition BOX**

| | |
|---|---|
| on | between |
| below | through |
| in | above |
| up | beside |
| with | down |
| under | into |
| to | off |
| along | over |
| by | |

**3** Choose three prepositions to write in sentences in your book.

# COMMON WORDS ›

**1** Choose words from the Spelling List to fill the gaps. Write the complete sentences in your book.

a. Michael's mother _ _ _ _ him to be careful.
b. I _ _ _ _ _ want to go to the market today.
c. Lila won the race by _ _ _ _ ten centimetres.
d. I asked if could go to the sing sing and Dad said, "_ _ _".
e. The big dog ran _ _ _ _ _ _ the corner.

**Spelling LIST**

around
don't
just
told
yes
calm
palm
tomato
banana
bath

**2** Write the words from the Spelling List with a silent 'l' in sentences in your book to show their meaning.

**Writing activity › Home Alone**

- Imagine you are at home all by yourself. Write about what could happen. It could be something scary or something adventurous. Make sure you include a beginning, a middle and an ending in your story.

Revision

# FOCUS > 'ow', 'oy' sounds

**1** Choose the letters 'ou' or 'ow' to fill the gaps in these words from Word Bank ①. Write the words in your book.

| | | | | | |
|---|---|---|---|---|---|
| s__ __nd | anyh__ __ | am__ __nt | w__ __ | c__ __ | sc__ __t |
| pr__ __l | all__ __ | c__ __nt | al__ __d | someh__ __ | p__ __nd |

**2** Choose two 'ow' words and two 'ou' words from Word Bank ①. Write them in sentences in your book.

**3** Copy these words into your book. Circle the odd one out and write it in a sentence.

| | | | | | |
|---|---|---|---|---|---|
| **a.** | cow | now | cloud | sow | wow |
| **b.** | crouch | pouch | slouch | round | couch |
| **c.** | anyhow | somehow | now | punch | cow |
| **d.** | background | ground | scout | sound | pound |

**4** Write the words from Word Bank ① in alphabetical order in your book.

**5** Choose the letters 'oy' or 'oi' to fill the gaps in these words from Word Bank ②. Write the words in your book.

| | | | | | |
|---|---|---|---|---|---|
| ch__ __ce | cowb__ __ | j__ __nt | b__ __ling | v__ __ce | j__ __n |
| t__ __ | v__ __d | p__ __nt | ann__ __ | j__ __ | c__ __n |
| av__ __d | destr__ __ | tomb__ __ | schoolb__ __ | | |

**6** Choose two 'oi' words and two 'oy' words from Word Bank ②. Write them in sentences in your book.

**7** Find a rhyming word for each of these words. Write each pair of words in your book.

toy voice joint coin toiling

**8** Copy these words into your book. Circle the odd one out and write it in a sentence.

| | | | | | |
|---|---|---|---|---|---|
| **a.** | boy | toy | scout | destroy | ahoy |
| **b.** | coil | found | foil | toil | boil |
| **c.** | schoolboy | tomboy | boiling | destroy | annoy |
| **d.** | boiling | toiling | coiling | foiling | annoying |

**Word BANK ①**

round
aloud
prowl
amount
cloud
somehow
scout
anyhow
eyebrow
count
scowl
sound
pound
allow
wow
cow

**Word BANK ②**

point
annoy
destroy
boiling
choice
voice
avoid
coin
cowboy
joy
void
tomboy
schoolboy
joint
join
toy

# FOCUS > 'air', 'ar' sounds

**1** Copy these tables. Write words from Word Bank ③ into the correct box.

Add two words of your own to the correct box.

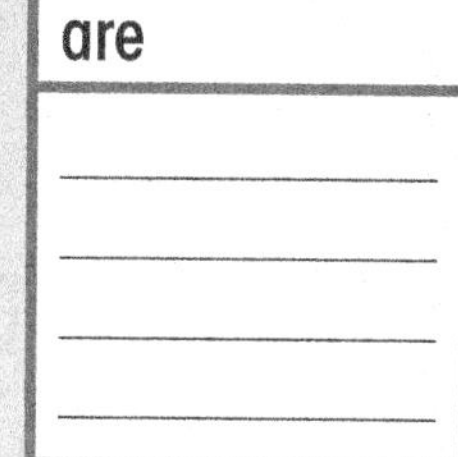


**✱ RULE**

Remember, a **homophone** is a word with the same sound as another word, but with different spelling and a different meaning, for example: *fair* and *fare*.

**Word BANK ③**

spare, air, fairy, bare, chair, beware, care, fair, flair, dare, lair, dairy, rare, wheelchair, funfair, hardware, pair, aware, unfair, square, stair, airport, airway, armchair, prepare

**2** Write sentences in your book to show the different meanings for these words.

fair fare bare bear pair pear stair stare

**3** There are five words in Word Bank ③ that begin with the letter '**a**'. Write them in alphabetical order in your book.

**4** Choose two '**a**' words and two '**ar**' words from Word Bank ④. Write them in sentences in your book.

**5** Choose the letters '**a**', '**al**' or '**ar**' to fill the gaps in these words from Word Bank ④. Write the words in your book.

| | | | | |
|---|---|---|---|---|
| sh__ __k | tom__to | c__ __m | c__ __f | b__sketball |
| h__ __f | gl__ss | c__ __port | p__ __k | f__ __ |
| m__sk | fl__sk | sp__ __k | p__ __m | __sk |

**Word BANK ④**

calm, spark, glass, basketball, starfish, park, carport, flask, palm, tomato, calf, mask, far, shark, ask, half

**6** Choose three '**ar**' words that are not in Word Bank ④. Write them in sentences in your book.

**7** Copy these words into your book. Circle the odd one out and write it in a sentence.

| | | | | | |
|---|---|---|---|---|---|
| **a.** | car | far | bar | fare | tar |
| **b.** | coin | glass | pass | mask | bath |
| **c.** | carpark | carport | carpet | cardboard | glasshouse |
| **d.** | classes | glasses | halves | cats | calves |
| **e.** | tomato | potato | palm | path | half |

**8** Write the words in Word Bank ④ in alphabetical order.

# FOCUS > 'u' sound (as in 'mug' / 'come')

**Word LIST**

mug, bug, come, some, rug, snug, done, none, thug, mud, undone, become, welcome, bud, gun, son, sun, stun, ton, love, bun, bunt, uncle, run, glove, bump, stun, rump, above, hunt, stunt, mother, brother, dust, rust, front, dull, tuck, luck, struck, stuck, bunch, hunch, munch, lunch

**1** Copy these words into your book.
Circle the odd one out and write it in a sentence.

| | | | | | |
|---|---|---|---|---|---|
| a. | truck | thug | some | same | mug |
| b. | become | snug | truck | track | mud |
| c. | rug | luck | dust | lack | none |
| d. | become | snug | snag | dove | dull |
| e. | shove | son | sun | sand | stun |
| f. | mother | none | every | hunt | hunch |

**2** Find the missing letters in these words from the Word List.
Write the complete words in sentences in your book.
The first one has been done for you.

ome → *come* *Please* ***come*** *to my place tomorrow.*

| | | |
|---|---|---|
| uck → ______ | abo → ______ | ust → ______ |
| unc → ______ | fro → ______ | wel → ______ |
| moth → ______ | dus → ______ | glo → ______ |

**3** Find the wrong letter in the underlined words in these sentences.
Change the letter and write the correct words in your book.
The first one has been done for you.

a. I lave to go swimming after school. → *love*
b. The man sold his banch of bananas at the market.
c. The car was travelling too fast and it hit the frent of the building.
d. Have you dune your homework yet?
e. My mother and brather like to go fishing on Saturdays.
f. Will the trock make it to the top of the steep hill?
g. The car ran over a large bamp in the road.
h. My mather got a fright.
i. We mast get home before it gets too dark.
j. The boys will hant for rabbits with a spear, not a gan.

**4** Find words from the Word List that have a similar meaning to these words. Write the words in sentences in your book. The first one has been done for you.

you wear this on your hand → *glove  I wear a glove on my hand.*

wet, squelchy dirt → m_ _ _

the opposite of back → f_ _ _t

your female parent → m_ _h_ _

to knock up against something → b_ _ _

**5** Choose a word from the Word Bank to complete these sentences.

**Word BANK**

hunch  mother  above  come  struck  must

a. My _ _ _ _ _ _ sells fish at the market.
b. The small boy was _ _ _ _ _ _ by the speeding car.
c. The bird flew high _ _ _ _ _ the trees.
d. Milo had a _ _ _ _ _ that we would be hiding under the bed.
e. Our friends will _ _ _ _ to town to meet us.
f. We _ _ _ _ tell Dad what happened at school today.

**6** Choose the correct word. Write the words in complete sentences in your book.

a. Joe likes to have (fan / fun) during class.
b. My friend will (come / done) to school today.
c. The car had lots of (dust / rust) and holes on its doors.
d. I would (love / dove) to learn how to play the guitar.
e. The small boy's shoelaces were (anyone / undone).
f. The (outcome / become) of the elections will be recorded in the newspaper.

**7** Find small words inside these words. Write each small word in a sentence in your book. The first one has been done for you.

become → *come  Will you come to my place tomorrow?*

brother → ______  bunch → ______  glove → ______  mother → ______

struck → ______  shunt → ______  undone → ______  thug → ______

done → ______  stunt → ______  stuck → ______

**Off the page**

- How many words from the Word List can you make using the letters in this box? You can use each letter as many times as you like. Try to make at least ten words.

u e g m p l o n h w c s

# WORD KNOWLEDGE › Question marks

**RULE**

A **question mark** is placed at the end of a sentence to show that the sentence is a question.
For example: *What is your name? Do you like chocolate?*

**1** Copy this story into your book. Circle the question marks.

**Amo's Birthday Party**
It was Amo's ninth birthday. He was excited because he was having a party.
All his friends were coming.
"What will we have to eat, Mum?" asked Amo.
"What games will we play, Dad?" he asked.
Amo asked, "What am I going to wear?"
"When will they be here?" he asked.
"What time is it?" Amo asked.
"Is that the door bell?" Amo yelled.
"Yippee! It's time for my party to start."

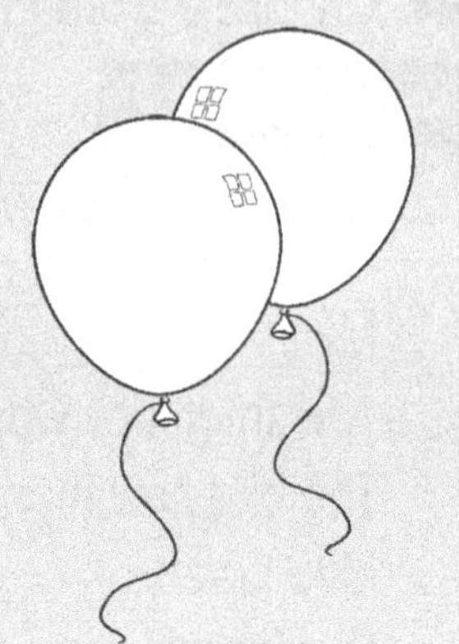

**2** Add a question mark or a full stop to these sentences.
Write the complete sentences in your book.

a. How old are you
b. It is cold today
c. What is the time
d. Can I come too
e. I don't know what you want

# COMMON WORDS ›

**1** Choose words from the Spelling List to fill the gaps.
Write the complete sentences in your book.

a. We went to the _ _ _ _ _ for a swim.
b. Our work must be _ _ _ _ _ _ _ _ before we go out to play.
c. The head man _ _ _ _ _ _ the pig for the feast.
d. We are going to the market _ _ _ _ _.
e. My dad told me a very _ _ _ _ _ joke.

**Spelling LIST**

today
beach
killed
finished
funny
done
undone
welcome
someone
anyone

**2** Write the two compound words from the Spelling List in your book.

**3** Write the smaller words in the compound words in sentences in your book.

**Writing activity › When I'm 25**

- Imagine that you are 25 years old. Write about what you might be doing. Think about these questions: What kind of job will I have? Where will I be living? Will I have my own family? What exciting adventures will I have?

## FOCUS › 'e' sound (as in 'let' / 'bread')

**Word LIST**

| | |
|---|---|
| let | leather |
| met | tread |
| bread | left |
| head | spent |
| bet | spend |
| set | melt |
| ready | bend |
| spread | send |
| wed | weather |
| thread | heavy |
| get | cent |
| jet | sent |
| pet | scent |
| dread | went |
| tread | headache |
| yet | lent |
| fret | rent |
| dress | headdress |
| kept | bent |
| ahead | headlight |
| overhead | pen |
| slept | headmaster |
| sunset | pencil |
| feather | yell |
| yellow | headphone |
| tent | sled |

**1** Copy these words into your book.
Circle the odd one out and write it in a sentence.

| | | | | | |
|---|---|---|---|---|---|
| a. | left | tent | head | hand | read |
| b. | ahead | thread | keep | instead | sent |
| c. | heavy | headache | lead | lad | yell |
| d. | feather | cent | scant | sent | instead |
| e. | bent | bunt | tread | fret | ahead |
| f. | weather | never | dread | headache | leather |

**2** Find the missing letters in these words from the Word List.
Write the complete words in sentences in your book.
The first one has been done for you.

ent → *spent* *I spent my money at the supermarket buying sweets.*

ten → ______ ead → ______ dre → ______ spe → ______

yel → ______ headd → ______ spre → ______ sle → ______

**3** Find the wrong letter in the underlined words in these sentences.
Change the letter and write the correct words in your book.
The first one has been done for you.

a. The <u>treed</u> on the tyre was very worn. → *tread*
b. The old man had a <u>feafher</u> in his headband.
c. Lima wore a <u>yellew</u> dress to school.
d. The dog <u>sleet</u> under the house
e. My ice cream will <u>malt</u> if I don't eat it quickly.
f. The bright flower had a strong <u>skent</u>.
g. Kila used a <u>pencel</u> to write the answers in her book.
h. The <u>weether</u> was so bad that we had to sleep in a <u>teet</u>.

**4** Find words from the Word List that have a similar meaning to these words.
Write the words in sentences in your book. The first one has been done for you.

a domestic animal → *pet* *I have a pet dog.*

a sore head → h_ _d_ _ _e

not straight → b_ _ _

you write with it → p_ _ _ _l

the colour of a lemon → _ _ll_ _

material made from animal skins → l_ _th_ _

## 5 Choose a word from the Word Bank to complete these sentences.

**Word BANK**

headmaster pen ahead headlight yellow headdress bend pencil hen

a. The road sign ______ says STOP.
b. The car's __________ was very bright.
c. Our __________ is a very tall man.
d. The ____ in the river was very narrow.
e. We can use a ___ or a ______ to do our schoolwork.
f. My pet ___ has ______ feathers.
g. The villager wore a colourful __________.

## 6 Choose the correct word. Write the words in complete sentences in your book.

a. The workman wore (feather / leather) gloves.
b. The workman fixed the (overhead / tread) power lines.
c. Mum will bake (read / bread) in the oven today.
d. Our teacher had a (headache / headphone) so she went home.
e. The baby pig will (wet / fret) if she is taken away from her mother.
f. The farmer will (spread / thread) the compost all over his garden.

## 7 Find small words inside these words. Write each small word in a sentence in a book. The first one is done for you.

bread → *read* *I read the story before I went to bed.*

ahead → ______ yellow → ______
sunset → ______ pencil → ______
scent → ______ thread → ______
headdress → ______ headphone → ______

**Off the page**

- How many words from the Word List can you make using the letters in this box? You can use each letter as many times as you like. Try to make at least ten words.

d e g m t l a n h w c p s o h

# WORD KNOWLEDGE > Exclamation marks

**RULE**

An **exclamation mark** is placed at the end of a sentence to show that the sentence is an exclamation. It shows happiness, excitement, anger or worry.
For example: *Ouch! I hit my thumb! Bad luck! Good work!*

Choose the best exclamation from the Exclamation Box for each speech bubble. Write the exclamations in your book.

**Exclamation BOX**

Stop that now!
I'm clever – I can do the splits!
I'll never get this homework done!
Ouch!

## COMMON WORDS >

**1** Choose words from the Spelling List to fill the gaps.
Write the complete sentences in your book.

a. I'm tired and I have a ________________.

b. I did my homework __________________ so it would be ready for today.

c. I found the ________ in the library.

d. You can find that information on a ________________.

e. The boy called the dog over ________.

**2** Write five words that begin with the word '**head**'.
Write them in your book.

**Spelling LIST**

book
here
things
yesterday
computer
headache
weather
spread
head
pencil

**Writing activity > Angry or Sad?**

- Write about a time when you were very angry or sad.
  Write about how you felt, what you did and said, and why you felt that way.
  Don't forget to include some exclamation marks in your writing!

# FOCUS › 'o' sound (as in 'hot' / 'was')

**Word LIST**

| | |
|---|---|
| hot | quarry |
| hog | knot |
| hole | holiday |
| was | hospital |
| what | wasp |
| hop | bottom |
| on | bottle |
| wash | cloth |
| washing | squash |
| cot | wallet |
| dog | wallaby |
| wander | moth |
| boss | robber |
| cross | rocket |
| wand | knock |
| swan | comic |
| lock | copy |
| block | squabble |
| swallow | hog |
| wonder | |

**1** Choose the letters 'o' or 'a' to fill the gaps in these words from the Word List. Write the words in your book.

| | | | | |
|---|---|---|---|---|
| sw__n | w__shing | w__sp | h__spital | wh__t |
| h__le | c__mic | cr__ss | h__t | l__ck |
| sw__llow | r__bber | w__s | h__liday | b__ttom |

**2** Find the wrong letter in the underlined words in these sentences. Change the letter and write the correct words in your book. The first one has been done for you.

a. I will wosh the car tomorrow.
b. The wasp bit her on her botton.
c. When the light went on the mofh flew into it.
d. If you are late the biss will be criss.
e. Next Saturday we begin our huliday.
f. The rubber crawled in through the window.
g. I wonder whot was wrong.
h. Lima could not swollow her vegetables.

**3** Find the missing letters in these words from the Word List. Write the complete words in sentences in your book. The first one has been done for you.

og → *hog* *Dad put the **hog** in the sty.*

| | | |
|---|---|---|
| bloc → ______ | walle → ______ | robb → ______ |
| sw → ______ | cop → ______ | rocke → ______ |
| walla → ______ | kn → ______ | squa → ______ |

**4** Copy these words into your book. Circle the odd one out and write it in a sentence.

| | | | | | |
|---|---|---|---|---|---|
| a. | hot | dog | swan | same | cloth |
| b. | rocket | pocket | socket | packet | locket |
| c. | knock | sock | sick | jockey | clock |
| d. | copy | cloth | cot | hop | class |
| e. | was | what | when | wander | wonder |
| f. | bottle | bottom | bonnet | roof | boss |

## 5 Choose a word from the Word Bank to complete these sentences.

**Word BANK**

hole lock wash squash knot squabble copy wallaby

a. Remember to _ _ _ _ the door when you go out.
b. The children started to shout and _ _ _ _ _ _ _ _ when the teacher left the room.
c. The small _ _ _ _ _ _ _ hopped across the road.
d. If you _ _ _ _ _ _ the tomatoes they will bruise.
e. Maria tried to _ _ _ _ the work from her friend.
f. There was a _ _ _ _ in the bucket and the water leaked out.
g. Don't forget to _ _ _ _ your hands before you eat.
h. Tie a _ _ _ _ in your shoelaces before you start running.

## 6 Choose the correct word. Write the words in complete sentences in your book.

a. It is too (hot / hold) to work today
b. The (swan / swallow) swam across the lake.
c. The (robber / boss) told the man to work harder.
d. Mum did not know (what / where) to do with the naughty cat.
e. I (was / were) going to the sing sing today.
f. The (bottle / wallet) is full of fizzy drink.

## 7 Use the clues to find the words in these puzzles. Write them in your book.

a. w
**Across:** a stinging insect
**Down:** you keep money in it

b. r
**Across:** a spacecraft
**Down:** someone who steals things

c. b
**Across:** a tall glass container
**Down:** the opposite of top

d. h ... d
**Across:** an animal that barks
**Down:** time off from work or school

e. h
**Across:** very warm
**Down:** a kind of pig

f. s
**Across:** to press something to make it flat
**Down:** a large water bird

### Off the page

- How many words from the Word List can you make using the letters in this box? You can use each letter as many times as you like. Try to make at least ten words.

c f a h n o v p g w s h t

# WORD KNOWLEDGE > Statements

**RULE**

A **statement** is a sentence that gives information about something.
A **statement** can describe what you feel or think about something.
For example: *I like reading. The dog found the bone.*

**1** Choose an ending from the Statement Box to complete these sentences. Write the complete sentences in your book.

a. The monkey ______________________.
b. The parrot ______________________.
c. The fish ______________________.
d. The rooster ______________________.
e. The pilot ______________________.
f. Pastor John ______________________.

**Statement BOX**

- flew the plane
- ate the bananas
- flew into the tree
- crowed very loudly
- is our minister
- swam away

**2** Write statements in your book to answer these questions.

a. What is the name of your village?
b. How many people are in your family?
c. What is your favourite animal?
d. What do you like to do on the weekend?

## COMMON WORDS >

**1** Choose words from the Spelling List to fill the gaps. Write the complete sentences in your book.

a. We _ _ _ _ old people to cross the road.
b. Marie made a sand _ _ _ _ _ _ at the beach.
c. We are going to the _ _ _ to see the lions.
d. The children's mother said to come inside _ _ _.
e. Lela likes to _ _ _ _ her bike to school.

**2** Write the words from the Spelling List with the silent 'k' in sentences in your book to show their meaning.

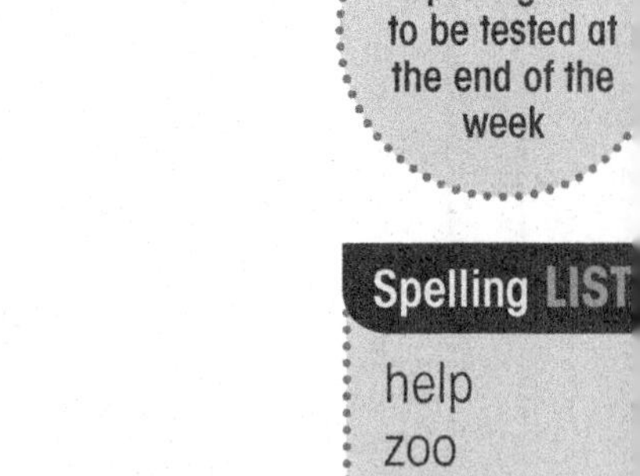

**Spelling LIST**

- help
- zoo
- now
- ride
- castle
- hospital
- knock
- knot
- wash
- what

**Writing activity > At the Sing Sing**

- Imagine that you meet someone who has never been to a sing sing. Write about what you wear and do. Write about the music and the dancing. Describe what you like best about sing songs.

## FOCUS > 'i' sound (as in 'bit' / 'gym')

**Word LIST**

| | |
|---|---|
| bit | gymnastics |
| hit | mystery |
| hymn | pyjamas |
| gym | spill |
| silly | prison |
| sister | synonym |
| quiz | homonym |
| wrist | antonym |
| quickly | fifty |
| kitchen | picnic |
| myth | insect |
| gypsy | symbol |
| window | Egypt |
| chicken | sixty |
| cricket | stick |
| river | gymnasium |
| chill | cryptic |

**1** Choose a word from the Word List for each picture.
Write the words in alphabetical order in your book.

f_f__ __

ch__ck__ __

gy__ __ __ __ __ __ __ __

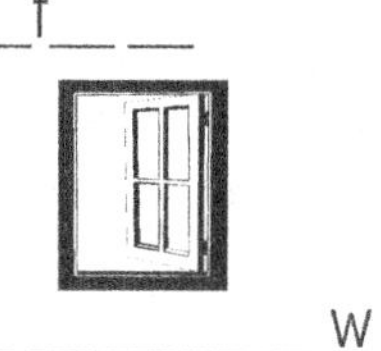

__ __ __ __ __w

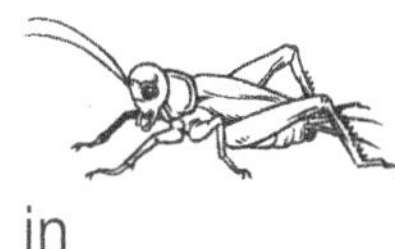

in__ __ __ __

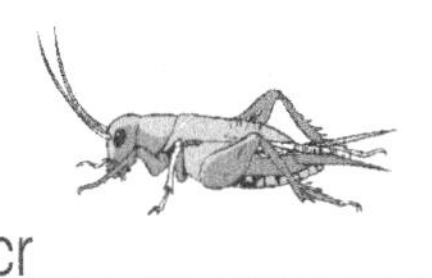

cr__ __ __ __ __

**2** Find the missing letters in these words from the Word List.
Write the complete words in sentences in your book.
The first one has been done for you.

uiz → *quiz* *I got all the answers right in the* ***quiz****.*

| | | |
|---|---|---|
| pris → ______ | quickl → ______ | gyp → ______ |
| Egy → ______ | iver → ______ | wri → ______ |
| ymn → ______ | ystery → ______ | fif → ______ |

**3** Find the wrong letter in the underlined words in these sentences.
Change the letter and write the correct words in your book.
The first one has been done for you.

**a.** My <u>soster</u> went to the market.
**b.** The robber was sent to <u>prisen</u>.
**c.** Tom's <u>pyjimas</u> have blue stripes.
**d.** Our family went for a <u>pucnic</u> yesterday.
**e.** Please close the <u>windew</u> before you go.
**f.** I wonder <u>whot</u> kind of present I will get.
**g.** We go to the <u>jym</u> to get fit.
**h.** The brown <u>chichen</u> laid an egg.

**4** Copy these words into your book.
Circle the odd one out and write it in a sentence.

| | | | | | |
|---|---|---|---|---|---|
| **a.** | hit | bit | win | happy | flip |
| **b.** | hymn | hymns | gym | gyms | hikes |
| **c.** | river | sister | blister | gentle | middle |
| **d.** | Egypt | symbol | gym | cycle | myth |
| **e.** | fifty | sixty | six | forty | fifth |
| **f.** | cricket | picket | wicket | tribe | thicket |

**5** Choose a word from the Word Bank to complete these sentences.

**Word BANK**

quiz wrist window spill insect bit hymn gym

a. The large dog ___ ___ ___ the small cat.
b. All the people in the church sang the ___ ___ ___ ___.
c. Be careful not to ___ ___ ___ ___ ___ your soup on the table.
d. We had a ___ ___ ___ ___ to see who knew the most.
e. The small ___ ___ ___ ___ ___ ___ flew into Simon's eye.
f. Loki broke her ___ ___ ___ ___ ___ when she fell out of the tree.
g. Simon went to the ___ ___ ___ to do his exercises.
h. The cricket ball went straight through the ___ ___ ___ ___ ___ ___.

**6** Choose the correct word. Write the words in complete sentences in your book.

a. The water from the (river / rider) flowed through the village.
b. Our dad likes to cook meat in the (bathroom / kitchen).
c. When you add twenty-five to twenty-five it makes (fifty / mystery).
d. The bully (hit / hid) the small boy on the arm.
e. Run (chicken / quickly) before they catch you.
f. Please do not be (silent / silly) when you are doing your homework.

**7** Use the clues to find the words in these puzzles. Write them in your book.

a. s p _ _ _ / s i _ _ _ _
**Across:** to tip liquid out
**Down:** not sensible

b. s t _ _ _ _
**Across:** a thin piece of wood
**Down:** one more than fifty-nine

c. p _ _ _ _ _ _
**Across:** criminals are sent here
**Down:** you wear these when you sleep

d. c _ _ _ _ _ _
**Across:** a sport played with a bat and ball
**Down:** an animal that lays eggs

e. s _ _ _ _ / f _ _ _ y
**Across:** 5 x 10
**Down:** 6 x 10

f. q u i _ _ _ _ / s i _
**Across:** moving fast
**Down:** to rest on your bottom

**Off the page**

- How many words from the Word List can you make using the letters in this box? You can use each letter as many times as you like. Try to make at least ten words.

d k y m v s j a r i m t d h

# WORD KNOWLEDGE > Speech marks

**RULE**

**Speech marks** are placed around words that are spoken.
For example: *"Hello," said Jenifa. "Can you get me a plate please?"*

**1** Copy these sentences into your book.
Add speech marks before and after what is being said.

a. Dad said, I want my dinner.
b. Mum said, It's time for bed.
c. The train driver shouted, All aboard!
d. Simon cried, Give that back!

**2** Copy this poem into your book. Add speech marks before and after what is being said.

*The big pig on the farm close by,*
*All by himself ran away from the sty.*
*The dog said, Woof!*
*The cow said, Moo!*
*The sheep said, Baa!*
*The dove said, Coo!*
*The big pig began to cry,*
*And as fast as he could he ran back to the sty.*

# COMMON WORDS >

**1** Choose words from the Spelling List to fill the gaps.
Write the complete sentences in your book.

a. The baby threw her __ __ __ out of the cot.
b. Lela __ __ __ __ __ to win, but she came second.
c. The children stayed with their __ __ __ __ __ __ __ during the holidays.
d. Michael said he wanted __ __ __ __ ice cream.
e. You have to __ __ __ __ very closely to see the tiny bird.

Weekly Spelling List to be tested at the end of the week

**Spelling LIST**

toy
cousins
look
more
tried
quiz
chill
gym
Egypt
prison

**2** The word '**gym**' is short for two longer words that are also in the Word List.
Write both words in sentences in your book.

**Writing activity > Write a Poem**

- Write a poem about another animal like the one above.
Don't forget to put in the speech marks.

Revision

# FOCUS > 'u', 'e' sounds

**1** Copy these tables. Write words from Word Bank ① into the correct box.

Add two words of your own to the correct box.

| o | u |
|---|---|
| | |
| | |
| | |
| | |

**✱ RULE**

Remember, a **homophone** is a word with the same sound as another word, but with different spelling and a different meaning, for example: *son* and *sun*.

**Word BANK ①**

| | |
|---|---|
| mug | sun |
| some | undone |
| snug | struck |
| done | above |
| rug | love |
| bump | dust |
| thug | ton |
| someone | bunch |
| mother | none |
| come | glove |
| dull | front |

**2** Write sentences in your book to show the different meanings for these words.

sun son some sum none nun

**3** There are five words in Word Bank ① that begin with **'s–'**. Write them in alphabetical order in your book.

**4** Copy these tables. Write words from Word Bank ② into the correct box.

Add two words of your own to the correct box.

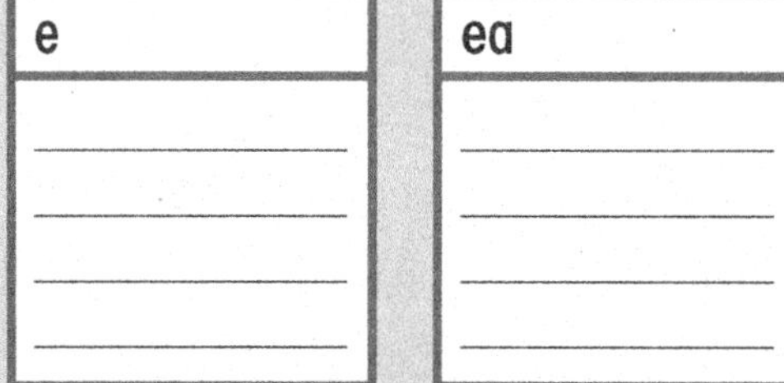

| e | ea |
|---|---|
| | |
| | |
| | |
| | |

**Word BANK ②**

| | |
|---|---|
| let | dress |
| spread | spent |
| leather | cent |
| bread | heavy |
| kept | feather |
| overhead | weather |
| scent | tread |
| dread | headach |
| spend | headligh |
| ready | bent |
| yellow | pencil |
| scent | |

**5** Copy this table into your book.
Fill the gaps to make rhyming words that follow the letter patterns.

| jetting | bread | send |
|---|---|---|
| w__tt______ | dr____d | b__nd |
| s__tt______ | spr______ | sp______ |
| b__tt______ | th________ | l______ |
| le____ing | h______ | dead-______ |
| ge__________ | d______ | m____d |
| | t________ | s______ |
| | | bl______ |

# FOCUS > 'o', 'i' sounds

**1** Choose the letter 'o' or 'a' to fill the gaps in these words from Word Bank ③. Write the words in your book.

| | | | | | |
|---|---|---|---|---|---|
| sw__n | w__nd | t__ssed | m__p | d__g | str__ng |
| p__t | cr__ss | w__tch | w__sh | l__ng | __ften |

**2** Write five of the complete words in sentences in your book.

**3** Write the words in the Word Bank that begin with 'w–' in alphabetical order in your book.

**✱ RULE**

Remember, an **antonym** is a word that means the opposite, for example: *hot* and *cold*.

**4** Choose an antonym from the Antonym Box for these words. Write each pair of words in your book.

| | | |
|---|---|---|
| top | colder | coldest |
| found | weak | weaker |
| hard | shorter | short |

**Antonym BOX**

stronger bottom hotter long soft
longer hottest strong lost

**Word BANK ③**

| | |
|---|---|
| pot | cold |
| mop | soft |
| want | wash |
| cross | fold |
| strong | wander |
| often | knot |
| was | bottom |
| wand | swap |
| watched | knock |
| wasn't | swan |
| long | watch |
| problem | tossed |
| dog | wonder |
| probably | |

**5** Choose the letter 'i' or 'y' to fill the gaps in these words from Word Bank ④. Write the words in your book.

| | | | | |
|---|---|---|---|---|
| m__ddle | l__ttle | c__ty | g__m | r__ddle |
| g__psy | f__ll | h__ll | sp__ll | m__th |

**6** Write five of the complete words in sentences in your book.

**7** Write all the words from the Word Bank that begin with 's–' in alphabetical order in your book.

**✱ RULE**

Remember, a **synonym** is a word that means the same, for example: *cold* and *chilly*.

**8** Choose a synonym from the Synonym Box for these words. Write each pair of words in your book.

| | | |
|---|---|---|
| stupid | fast | jail |
| cold | puzzle | stream |
| opposite | similar | slap |

**Synonym BOX**

quickly prison chilly silly quiz
river antonym synonym hit

**Word BANK ④**

| | |
|---|---|
| middle | sister |
| gym | sixty |
| little | Egypt |
| silly | fill |
| winter | spill |
| hill | picnic |
| city | pyjamas |
| synonym | myth |
| symbol | wrist |
| riddle | chicken |
| gypsy | |

# Unit 31

## FOCUS > 'c' sound (as in 'clown' / 'king' / 'back')

**1** Choose the letters 'c', 'k' or 'ck' to fill the gaps in these words from the Word List. Write the words in your book.

| | | | |
|---|---|---|---|
| __ing | __lown | __ite | __angaroo |
| __idnap | ti__ __et | __amel | clo__ __ |
| __amp | __omb | so__ __ | lo__ __ |
| __oala | __abbage | __elp | |

**2** Write five of the complete words in sentences in your book.

**3** Find words from the Word List that have a similar meaning to these words. Write the words in the word frames. The first one has been done for you.

a. c l o w n — a circus performer

b. to have good luck

c. to carry off someone

d. 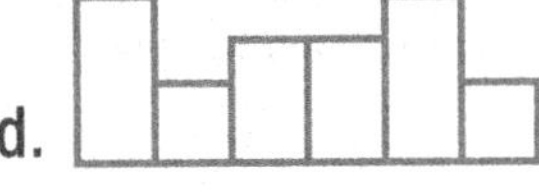 used to boil water

e. a game with bat, ball and wickets

f. you wear these on your legs

**4** Find rhyming words for these words. Write each pair of words in your book.

tack ramp pick luck wicket bite help pocket settle lock frown ring

**5** Change one letter in each word to make a new word. Write the new words in your book. The first one has been done for you.

a. t r i c k / b r i c k

b. t r a c k

c. l i c k

d. c l o c k

### Word LIST

| | |
|---|---|
| clown | capital |
| king | kidnap |
| back | rocket |
| camp | cabbage |
| kitten | comb |
| stick | block |
| carpet | kilogram |
| castle | kelp |
| kitchen | lucky |
| koala | checked |
| cricket | kite |
| stockings | camel |
| colour | sock |
| country | clock |
| kettle | calm |
| kangaroo | truck |
| ticket | brick |
| pocket | lock |

**6** Write as many words as you can in your book, using the magic word machines.
Write the words in your book under the correct heading.

a. 'c–' words

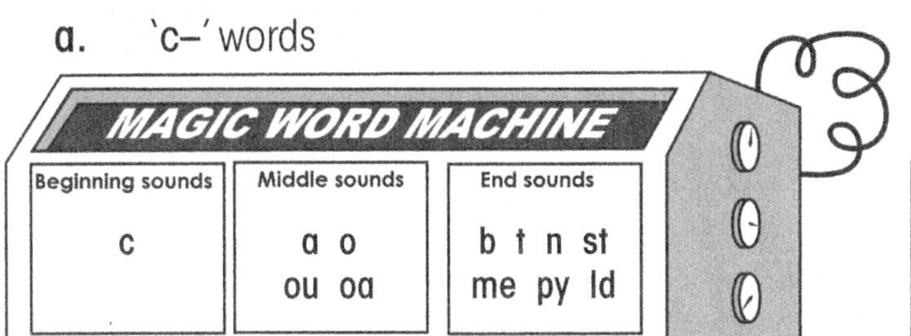


b. 'k–' words

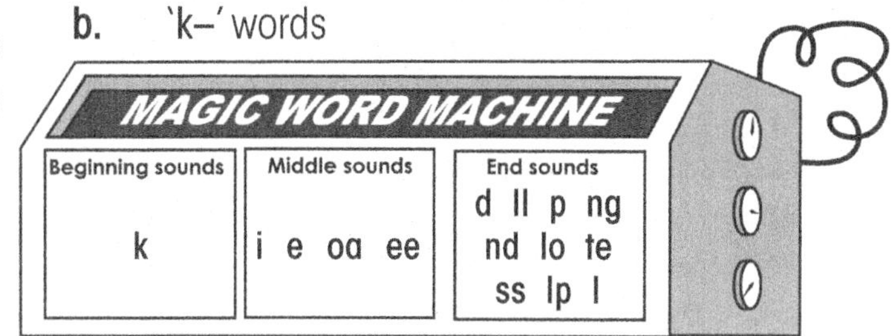


c. '–ck' words

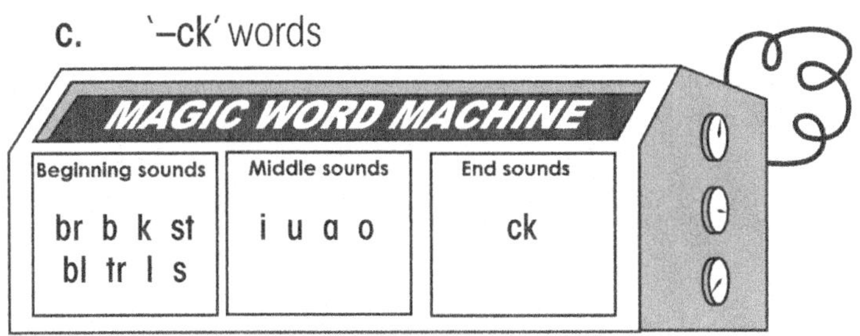


**7** Choose words from the Word List to complete these sentences.
Write the complete sentences in your book.

a. The tomatoes weighed exactly one ________________.
b. The bus driver ______________ the tickets as we got on the bus.
c. Port Moresby is the ______________ of Papua New Guinea.
d. Dad spilt a sticky drink on the ______________ floor.
e. I put my money in my ____________.

**8** Copy these words into your book. Circle the odd one out and write it in a sentence.

| | | | | | |
|---|---|---|---|---|---|
| a. | calf | camp | keep | cage | cow |
| b. | kid | king | kite | country | kitchen |
| c. | cricket | pocket | kidnap | lucky | packet |
| d. | trick | truck | track | trike | brick |

**9** Copy this crossword in your book. Write the correct word for each clue and find the mystery word.
Write the mystery word in a sentence in your book.

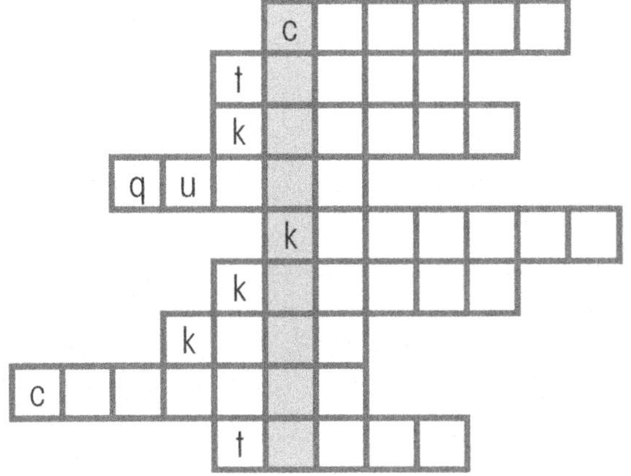


... kings and queens live in this
... a large vehicle
... a baby cat
... the opposite of slow
... a room for cooking
... a house for a dog
... it flies in the sky
... a baby hen
... to play a joke on someone

# WORD KNOWLEDGE › Speech marks

**RULE**

Remember, **speech marks** are placed around words that are spoken.
They show the exact words that someone has spoken and always appear in pairs, for example: "*I like jumping.*"

**1** Copy these sentences into your book.
Add speech marks before and after what is being said.

a. How are you?
b. Look at that.
c. Not now.
d. Come over here.
e. Get it quickly!
f. Wait a minute.

**2** Copy these sentences in your book. Underline the words that are spoken and add speech marks.
The first one has been done for you.

a. I fell off the wall, cried the boy. → "I fell off the wall," cried the boy.
b. Someone ate the chocolate, said Dad.
c. Kick it through the goal posts, shouted the coach.
d. Stay in after school, said the teacher.
e. I can't find my pen, wailed the child.
f. John said, I have lost my wallet.
g. The little boy cried, I want my mummy.

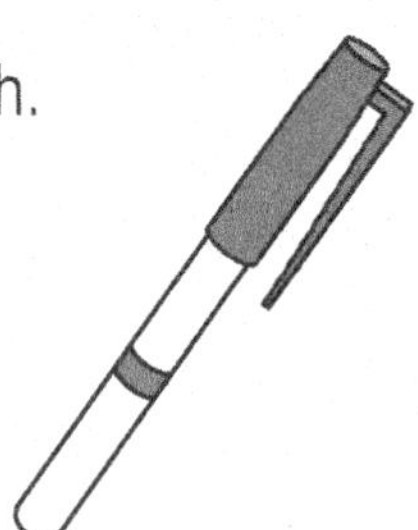

## COMMON WORDS ›

**1** Choose words from the Spelling List to fill the gaps.
Write the complete sentences in your book.

a. The story ended and they all lived _ _ _ _ _ _ _ ever after.
b. _ _ _ going to the market tomorrow.
c. My little brother is turning _ _ _ _ years old tomorrow.
d. The boat _ _ _ _ _ _ _ after we repaired the engine.
e. I would like to _ _ _ _ some treasure on this island.

**2** The words '**calm**', '**comb**' and '**castle**' all have a silent letter.
Write these words in your book and circle the silent letters.

**Spelling LIST**

find
four
I'm
happily
started
castle
calm
comb
rocket
kettle

**Writing activity › A Talking Story**

- Write a story of your own or retell a story that you know.
In your story, make sure that some of your characters talk to each other.
Don't forget to add speech marks around words that are spoken.

# FOCUS › 'j' sound (as in 'jug' / 'giraffe')

**Word LIST**

| | |
|---|---|
| jam | jetty |
| giraffe | Germany |
| jab | ginger |
| jet | gym |
| jug | jacket |
| giant | jigsaw |
| jazz | jumper |
| jelly | jawbone |
| cage | vegetables |
| page | garage |
| joke | cabbage |
| voyage | January |
| June | joy |
| July | magician |
| magic | stranger |
| gypsy | danger |
| jewels | angel |

**1** Choose the letters '**j**' or '**g**' to fill the gaps in these words from the Word List. Write the words in your book.

| | | | |
|---|---|---|---|
| __et | __elly | __ug | __igsaw |
| __iraffe | __iant | ma__ician | ve__etables |
| ca__e | __une | __ypsy | __ewels |

**2** Sort these words into groups by the sound that the letter '**g**' makes. Write the groups in your book.

go stranger get angel angry danger grab giant magic grunt

**3** Copy this table into your book.
Sort the words from the Word List into the correct box.

| 'g' makes a 'j' sound |
|---|
| |

| 'j' makes a 'j' sound |
|---|
| |

**4** Write all the words where the '**g**' makes a '**j**' sound in sentences in your book.

**5** Find rhyming words for these words. Write each pair of words in your book.

ham page belly poke boy stranger packet mug petty hymn bumper cab

**6** Choose the correct word. Write the words in complete sentences in your book.

a. The thief stole the (jewels / jawbone) from the safe.
b. The (cage / page) was too small for the lion.
c. The (magician / gymnast) made the rabbit disappear.
d. You should eat (jigsaws / vegetables) every day.
e. The (giraffe / gypsy) ate the leaves at the top of the tree.
f. The thief hid the (jewels / angels) under the house.
g. The small boy finished the (jigsaw / voyage) quickly.

**7** Choose words from the Word List to complete these sentences.

a. Dad parked the car in the _ _ _ _ _ _.
b. The first month of the year is _ _ _ _ _ _ _.
c. Michael broke his _ _ _ _ _ _ _ when he was playing football.
d. The _ _ _ _ _ tree crashed to the ground.
e. This _ _ _ _ _ _ puzzle is hard to solve.
f. The beautiful yacht began its _ _ _ _ _ _ _.

**8** Find words from the Word List in these lines of letters.
Write them in your book. The first one has been done for you.

a. b c k j e l l y l b j a z z c j o k e s m j o y → *jelly, jazz, joke, joy*
b. x v a n g e l v q r d a n g e r s t i g i a n t v
c. p j a c k e t u s v m j o c k e y z z v j u m p e r
d. g g g i n g e r g h i g y m g p m a g i c i a n g t s
e. d v r p a g e r v i c a g e z g a r a g e n v s t a g e s v n

**9** Copy these words into your book. Circle the odd one out and write it in a sentence.

| | | | | | |
|---|---|---|---|---|---|
| a. | jewels | jetty | jumper | jacket | cousin |
| b. | angel | games | giant | page | cage |
| c. | June | July | August | January | |
| d. | vegetables | fruit | garage | gypsy | stage |
| e. | magic | magical | clown | magician | |

**10** Copy this crossword in your book. Write the correct word for each clue and find the mystery word.
Write the mystery word in a sentence in your book.

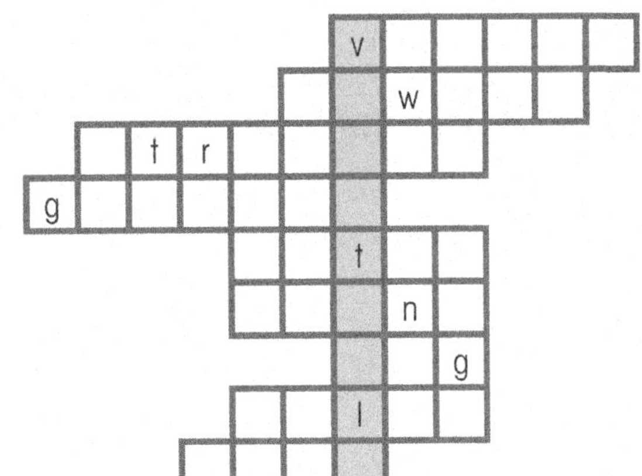


... a long journey
... precious stones
... a person you do not know
... an animal with a long neck
... you tie your boat to it
... a very tall, large person
... a paper or plastic container to carry things
... it wobbles and you eat it
... the sixth month of the year

# WORD KNOWLEDGE > Plurals

**RULE**

Some words stay the same whether they are singular or **plural**, for example: *sheep*.
I saw *one sheep* jump over the fence.
The farmer loaded *ten sheep* into the truck.

**1** Copy these sentences into your book. Use the Plural Box to find the word that stays the same for the singular and plural. Write the words in your book.

a. The Christmas sleigh was pulled by _ _ _ _ _ _ _ _.
b. We went to Lae to see the _ _ _ _ _ _ _ _.
c. The _ _ _ _ _ _ swam up the river to the sea.
d. The _ _ _ _ _ ran towards the open gate.
e. The _ _ _ _ swam away when the shark came near.

**Plural BOX**

fish
sheep
reindeer
salmon
aircraft
shears
tongs
tweezers
pliers
trousers

**2** Write these words in sentences to show the plural. tweezers pliers

**3** Write these words in sentences to show the singular. trousers tongs

# COMMON WORDS >

**1** Choose words from the Spelling List to fill the gaps.
Write the complete sentences in your book.

a. I saw the _ _ _ _ _ _ run across the paddock.
b. The _ _ _ _ _ _ breathed fire through its nostrils.
c. We are going out to play in _ _ _ _ minutes.
d. Dad asked the shopkeeper how _ _ _ _ the bananas cost.
e. When we reached the end of the road we _ _ _ _ _ _ the corner.

**2** Five of the words in the Spelling List have double letters.
Write these words in sentences in your book.

**3** Choose the words in the Spelling List where the letter '**g**' makes a 'j' sound.
Write them in sentences in your book.

**Spelling LIST**

dragon
much
rabbit
five
turned
giraffe
jelly
cabbage
magic
jetty

**Writing activity > What Makes You Proud?**

- What have you done that makes you feel really proud?
It could be something really kind or special that you did for a friend, your parents or another person.
- Write three or more sentences about what you have done.

# FOCUS › 's' sound (as in 'sun' / 'circle')

**Word LIST**

sun
circle
six
palace
sale
sang
cent
cycle
rice
fence
somebody
sometime
nice
place
circus
soap
sent
seventy
celery
centipede
twice
Saturday
sandwich
parcel
police
cement
piece
decide
silly
silent
voice
bicycle
mice

**1** Choose the letters '**s**' or '**c**' to fill the gaps in these words from the Word List. Write the words in your book.

| | | | | |
|---|---|---|---|---|
| __un | fen__e | __entipede | pala__e | __oap |
| __andwich | bi__ycle | __eventy | poli__e | __ent |

**2** Sort these words into groups by the sound that the letter '**c**' makes. Write the groups in your book.

cent cat centipede cycle cub celery clap count circus cross

**3** Copy this table into your book.
Sort the words from the Word List into the correct box.

| 'c' makes an 's' sound |
|---|
| |

| 's' makes an 's' sound |
|---|
| |

**4** Write all the words where the '**c**' makes an '**s**' sound in sentences in your book.

**5** Find rhyming words for these words. Write each pair of words in your book.

nice race hilly rang pale fix come choice

**6** Choose the correct word.
Write the words in complete sentences in your book.

a. We cooked some (rice / twice) to have for dinner.
b. The (parcel / centipede) crawled up the pipe.
c. This is a very (nice / silly) garden.
d. Simon saw the (sandwich / police) chase the criminal.
e. I will (celery / cycle) to your place tomorrow.

**7** Choose words from the Word List to complete these sentences.

a. We used _ _ _ _ to clean the dirty shelf.
b. My grandfather will be _ _ _ _ _ _ _ years old on Saturday.
c. We went to the _ _ _ _ _ _ to see where the king and queen lived.
d. My sister _ _ _ _ a song at the sing sing.
e. I am going to eat a _ _ _ _ _ _ _ _ for my lunch today.

**8** Find words from the Word List in these lines of letters.
Write them in your book. The first one has been done for you.

a. z f y <u>f e n c e</u> k v m <u>p a l a c e</u> e e <u>c e l e r y</u> u n <u>s u n</u> → *fence, palace, celery, sun*
b. b b c c b i c y c l e p o v p o l i c e r w a r i c e t t w t w i c e v x
c. v x w s i l e n t t t b k q s i l l y S a t u r d a y a n t s a n g v t l k
d. e m v c e m e n t t u r n i c e n f c y c l e d a u g s a l e n m p
e. a b c d e c i d e u w v o i c e s o a p p p a r c e l r s u t v l y n

**9** Copy these words into your book. Circle the odd one out and write it in a sentence.

| | | | | | |
|---|---|---|---|---|---|
| a. | circle | cycle | cent | danger | circus |
| b. | piece | price | lace | space | jigsaw |
| c. | somebody | somehow | nowhere | sometime | someplace |
| d. | silent | jacket | silly | seventy | sang |
| e. | bicycle | cycle | motorcar | tricycle | unicycle |

**10** Copy this crossword in your book. Write the correct word for each clue and find the mystery word.
Write the mystery word in a sentence in your book.

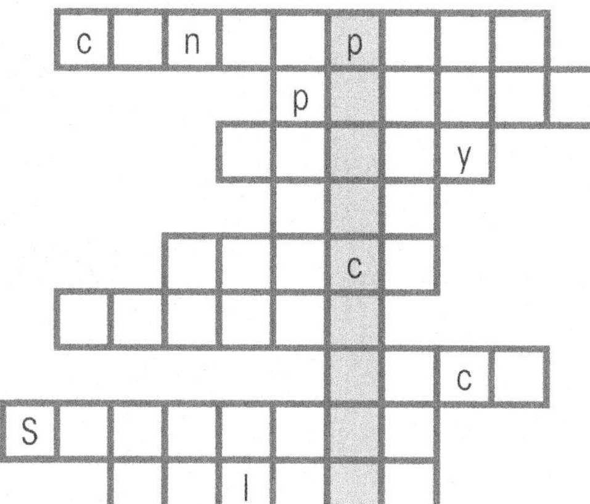


... a small creature with many legs
... they catch criminals
... stupid or foolish
... three plus three equals...
... you speak with this
... kings and queens live here
... the plural of mouse
... the day after Friday
... very quiet, no noise

# WORD KNOWLEDGE > Compound verbs

**RULE**

A **verb** is an **action** word that tells us what someone or something is doing, for example: *peep, jump*.
If an action has **already happened**, you use the **past tense** of the verb, for example: *peeped, jumped*.
If an action is happening **now**, you use the **present tense** of the verb, for example: *peeping, jumping*.
**Compound verbs** are made up of more than one word, for example: *I will be going to school soon.*

**1** Choose the right verb to fill the gap. Write the complete sentences in your book.

a. Simon (read, borrowed, kicked) the football.
b. The teacher (play, told, tripped) us to go inside.
c. My dad (drove, walked, found) the car to the market.
d. The horse (laughed, galloped, pushed) down the hill.

**2** Choose compound verbs from the Compound Verb Box to fill the gaps. Write the complete sentences in your book.

a. Mum __________ with us to the sing sing.
b. Lela __________ her new bilum.
c. The farmer __________ a new shed for the pigs.
d. The teacher said, "I __________ early tomorrow."
e. Michael said that they __________ for Lae next week.

**Compound Verb BO**

is building
will be coming
is going
will be leaving
has lost

## COMMON WORDS >

**1** Choose words from the Spelling List to fill the gaps. Write the complete sentences in your book.

a. I will _ _ _ _ a chocolate cake for my sister's birthday.
b. When the woodchopper cut down the tree, wood _ _ _ _ _ flew everywhere.
c. We are staying with my _ _ _ _ _ _ _ on the weekend.
d. Dad said that we could buy the watermelon on _ _ _ _ _ _ _ day.
e. We all ate our _ _ _ _ _ _ _ _ _ very early this morning.

**2** Write the words '**bicycle**', '**tricycle**' and '**cycle**' in sentences in your book to show the different meanings.

Weekly Spelling List to be tested at the end of the week

**Spelling LIST**

another
make
cousins
breakfast
chips
circus
somebody
seventy
parcel
bicycle

**Writing activity > What Happened Next?**

■ Imagine that you went into a stranger's garden to fetch a ball that you kicked there. Before you reached the ball, a giant dog jumped out at you. Write about what happened next. Include lots of action words in your story.

# Unit 34

## FOCUS › 'z' sound (as in 'zoo' / 'says' / 'present')

**1** Choose the letters 'z' or 's' to fill the gaps in these words from the Word List. Write the words in your book.

__ebra pri__on tiger__ apple__ __ip
pre__ent qui__ __oo __ero

**2** Sort these words into groups by the sound that the letter 's' makes: 'z' or 's'. Write the groups in your book.

span tigers sad nose story stop apples
song rulers start papers salt chisel zoo

**3** Copy this table into your book.
Sort the words from the Word List into the correct box.

| 's' makes a 'z' sound | 'z' makes a 'z' sound |
|---|---|
| | |

**4** Find rhyming words for these words. Write each pair of words in your book.

fizz hose fizzle as fuzz frizzy

**5** Choose the correct word.
Write the words in complete sentences in your book.

a. The (zebra / lion) has black and white stripes.
b. Lani could not do up the (zipper / zinc) in her tent.
c. She broke her (rose / nose) while playing softball.
d. If you do the crime you could go to (prison / present).
e. The (lazy / busy) people were asleep beside the road.

### Word LIST

zoo
as
is
zip
whizz
busy
prison
zoom
present
quiz
zero
dizzy
chisel
zebra
zipper
zigzag
resident
president
zap
zinc
rulers
papers
zest
zone
grizzle
apples
sizzle
has
tigers
zucchini
lazy
nose
buzz
chasm

**6** Choose words from the Word List to fill the gaps.
Write the complete sentences in your book.

a. I could hear the bee _ _ _ _ _ as it flew near my ear.
b. We use _ _ _ _ _ _ _ _ to draw straight lines in our books.
c. When I put the fish in the hot pan it began to _ _ _ _ _ _ _.
d. I gave my mother a _ _ _ _ _ _ _ _ _ for her birthday.
e. We saw the _ _ _ _ _ _ at the zoo.

**7** Find words from the Word List in these lines of letters.
Write them in your book. The first one has been done for you.

a. c m v <u>b u s y</u> k y v w <u>p r e s i d e n t</u> j <u>s i z z l e</u> b n <u>t i g e r s</u> w z s
→ *busy, president, sizzle, tigers*
b. z z s s z i g z a g v v w k z i n c t m z p q u i z s n r p r i s o n t m v
c. a b u z z c h a s m t y z a p p c h i s e l l m m m z o o m t s q r
d. y x w t z o o m a s b i s k k p r e s e n t t y v z o n e x z m n t
e. z i p s s s s p c h i s e l m k p r e s i d e n t v w d i z z y c f k

**8** Copy this crossword in your book. Write the correct word for each clue and find the mystery word.
Write the mystery word in a sentence in your book.

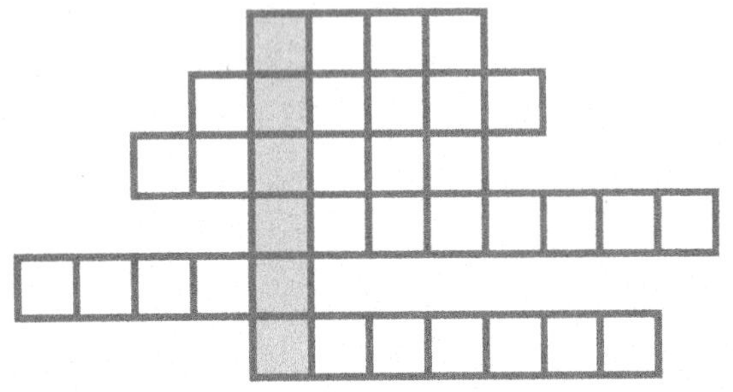

... nothing; the number 0
... a fastener for trousers and dresses
... wild cats with yellow and black stripes
... a long thin green vegetable
... an animal with black and white stripes
... to complain or whine

**RHYME time** › Copy this rhyme into your book and then ...

1. Circle all the words beginning with '**z–**'.
2. Underline all the words with the double '**ss**' letters.
3. Draw a square around the words where '**s**' says '**z**'.

*Zebra zebra, the road he is crossing.*
*Zebra zebra, be careful!*
*Zebra zebra, when you cross busy roads...*
*Use the zebra crossing.*

# WORD KNOWLEDGE › Compound nouns

**✱ RULE**

Remember, a **noun** is the name of a person, place or thing, for example: *cat, dog, garden*.
A **compound noun** is made when two or more smaller nouns are joined together to make a bigger one, for example: *bedroom, mousetrap*.

**1** Copy this table into your book. Use nouns to fill the gaps.
The first line has been done for you.

| animals | tiger | lion | cuscus |
|---|---|---|---|
| birds | | | |
| toys | | | |
| insects | | | |
| body parts | | | |

**2** Write the two smaller words that make up each of the compound nouns in the Compound Noun Box. For example, boyfriend = boy + friend

**3** Write sentences in your book for the two words in 'farmyard' and 'railway.'

**Compound Noun BOX**

boyfriend
mousetrap
bedroom
schoolboy
railway
waterfall
farmyard
girlfriend
paintbrush
wheelchair

## COMMON WORDS ›

**1** Choose words from the Spelling List to fill the gaps.
Write the complete sentences in your book.

a. After dinner we will go for a _ _ _ _ in the bush.
b. I saw a _ _ _ _ _ big cassowary today.
c. My dad and I went to the market _ _ _ _ _ _ _ _.
d. At the end of the year we gave our teacher a _ _ _ _ _ _ _.
e. The old man _ _ _ _ _ _ _ _ get up all the stairs.

**Spelling LIST**

couldn't
present
together
walk
great
zone
quiz
nose
busy
papers

**2** Write the four words from the Spelling List where the letter '**s**' makes a '**z**' sound in your book.

**Writing activity › What's Your Opinion?**

- Do you think making animals perform in a circus is a good thing?
- Say whether you agree or not and then write at least three sentences supporting your point of view.

Revision

## FOCUS › 'c', 'j' sounds

**1** Choose the letter 'c' or 'k' to fill the gaps in these words from Word Bank ①. Write the words in your book.

| | | | |
|---|---|---|---|
| __lown | __itten | __oala | __ettle |
| __omb | __ite | __astle | __ios__ |
| __idney | __alf | __iss | __angaroo |

**2** Write all the words from Word Bank ① that begin with the letter 'c' in sentences in your book.

**✱ RULE**

Remember, an **antonym** is a word that means the opposite, for example: *hot* and *cold*.
Remember, a **synonym** is a word that means the same, for example: *cold* and *chilly*.

**3** Choose an antonym from the Antonym Box for these words. Write each pair of words in your book.

| | | |
|---|---|---|
| front | hot | can |
| going | could | lucky |
| release | kind | went |

**Antonym BOX**

unlucky back came cold can't
couldn't capture unkind coming

**4** Choose the letter 'j' or 'g' to fill the gaps in these words from Word Bank ②. Write the words in your book.

| | | | |
|---|---|---|---|
| __ot | __iant | cabba__e | ma__ic |
| __ypsy | __etty | ve__etables | __uggle |
| __ewel | lu__ __a__e | | |

**5** Write the words where 'g' makes the 'j' sound in sentences in your book.

**6** Choose a synonym from the Synonym Box for these words.

| | | |
|---|---|---|
| monster | rubbish | soft |
| happiness | gemstones | bug |
| puzzle | leap | huge |
| trouble | | |

**Synonym BOX**

giant joy danger jigsaw magic jewels
jump junk joy gentle germ gigantic

**Word BANK ①**

kitten
kangaroo
kettle
kiss
castle
clown
comb
kiosk
koala
kite
kidney
calf

**Word BANK ②**

jot
gymnastics
jetty
jump
jewel
juggle
gypsy
vegetables
magic
giant
luggage
cabbage

# FOCUS ›. 's', 'z' sounds

**1** Choose the letter 's' or 'c' to fill the gaps in these words from Word Bank ③. Write the words in your book.

| | | | | |
|---|---|---|---|---|
| on__e | __i__ter | __un__et | gro__er | __y__le |
| __ir__ular | __ea__ick | fen__e | poli__e | pla__e |

**2** Write all the words where 'c' says 's' in sentences in your book.

**✻ RULE**

Remember, a **homophone** is a word with the same sound as another word, but with different spelling and a different meaning, for example: *sent* and *cent*.

**3** Write sentences in your book to show the different meanings for these words.

| | | | |
|---|---|---|---|
| sum → ______ | cell → ______ | cereal → ______ | saw → ______ |
| some → ______ | sell → ______ | serial → ______ | sore → ______ |

**4** Choose an antonym from the Antonym Box for these words. Write each pair of words in your book.

| | | |
|---|---|---|
| dry | useful | clever |
| certain | buy | hard |
| war | take | well |

**Antonym BOX**

sick silly sell peace juicy
uncertain useless receive soft

**5** Choose the letter 'z' or 's' to fill the gaps in these words from Word Bank ④. Write the words in your book.

| | | | | |
|---|---|---|---|---|
| si__ __le | whi__ __ | __ipper | __ucchini | __ebra |
| cho__en | chi__el | bu__y | pre__ent | qui__ |

**6** Write all the words where 's' makes the 'z' sound in sentences in your book.

**7** Choose a synonym from the Synonym Box for these words. Write each pair of words in your book.

| | | |
|---|---|---|
| snout | nought | hum |
| fastener | jail | test |
| active | wildlife park | gift |

**Synonym BOX**

zip busy zoo nose buzz
present zero quiz prison

**Word BANK ③**

once
grocer
fence
sentence
saucer
cycle
sunset
police
circular
place
seasick
sister

**Word BANK ④**

present
busy
quiz
zebra crossing
sizzle
whizz
zipper
chisel
zucchini
prayers
chosen

## FOCUS › 'i' (igh) sound (as in 'high' / 'light')

**Word LIST**

high
tight
fight
sigh
night
highlight
highlands
right
light
highway
flight
bright
knight
sight
might
fright
slight
frighten
thigh
bight
alright

**✱ RULE**

The long '**i**' sound can be shown by '**igh**' with a silent '**gh**'.
You need to remember what these words look like when you spell them.

**1** Choose a word from the Word List for each picture.
Write the words in alphabetical order in your book.

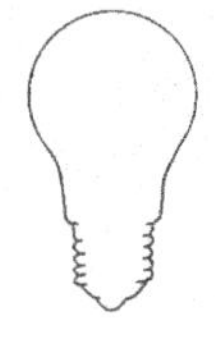
l_ _ _t

fr_ _ _t

s_ _ _

h_ _ _way

kn_ _ _t

h_ _ _

**2** Find words from the Word List that have a similar meaning to these words.
Write the words in the word frames. The first one has been done for you.

a. 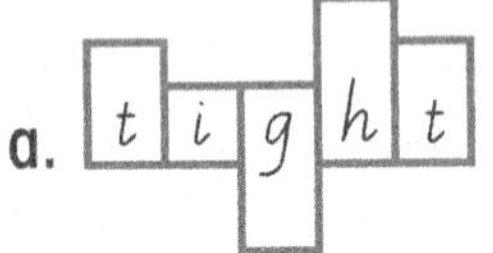

fitting very closely

b. 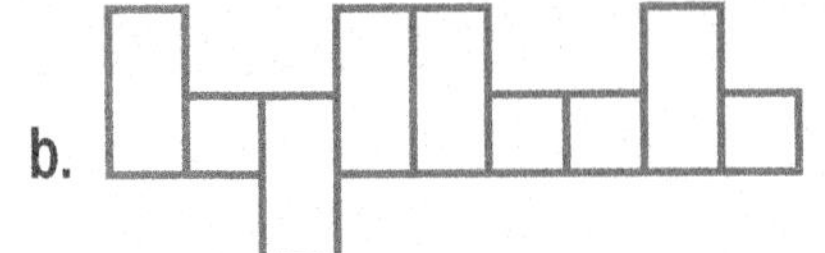
mountainous country in Papua New Guinea

c. 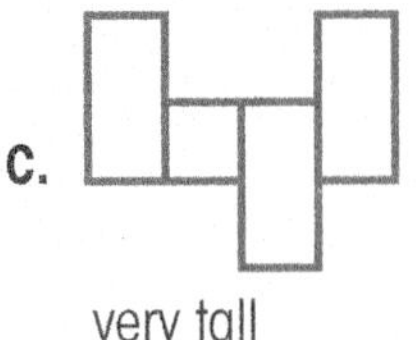
very tall

d. 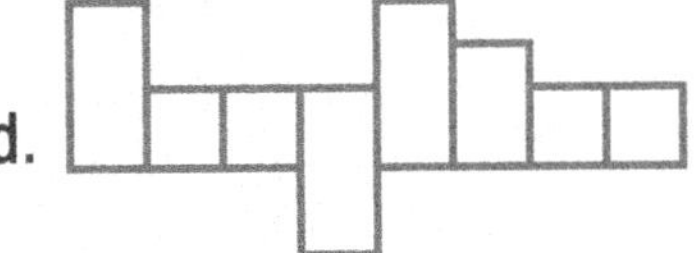
to make someone afraid

e. 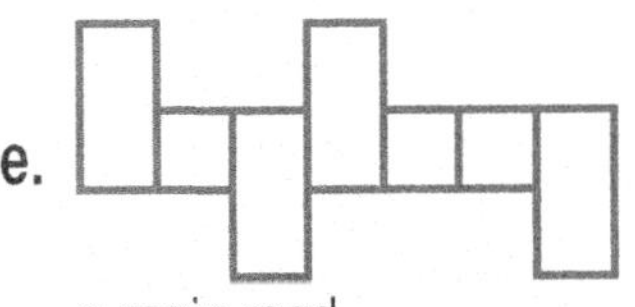
a main road

f. 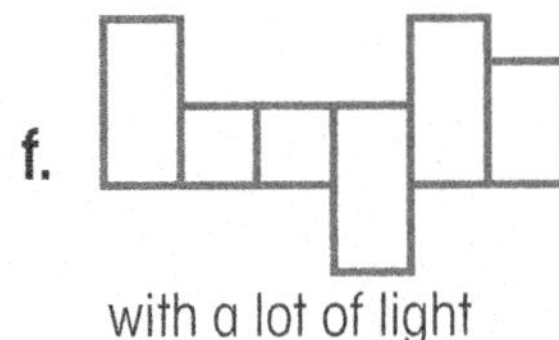
with a lot of light

**3** Choose words from the Word List to complete these sentences.
Write the complete sentences in your book.

a. You should look to the left and _ _ _ _ _ before crossing the road.
b. Dad said that we _ _ _ _ _ be able to go to the show tomorrow.
c. We play sport at _ _ _ _ _ under a _ _ _ _ _.
d. The stars were very _ _ _ _ _ _.
e. Mum let out a _ _ _ _ when she sat down.

**4** Find the difference in meaning between 'night' and 'knight'.
Write each word in a sentence in your book to show its meaning.

**5** Write as many words as you can in your book, using the magic word machine.

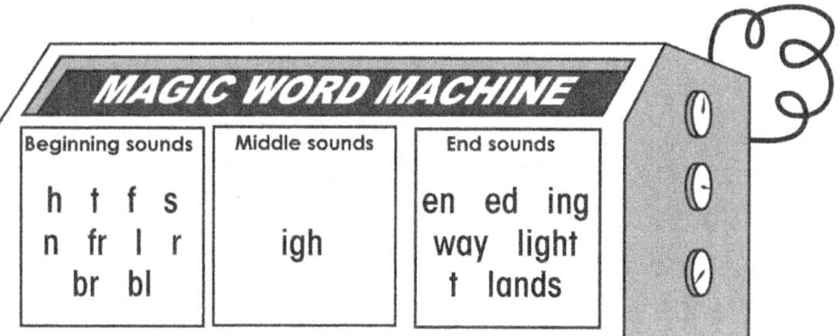


**6** Copy these words into your book.
Circle the odd one out and write it in a sentence.

| | | | | | |
|---|---|---|---|---|---|
| a. | light | bite | might | sight | bight |
| b. | high | highway | highlight | lowland | highlands |
| c. | fighting | lighting | frightening | brightening | time |
| d. | right | wrong | bright | fright | knight |

**7** Choose the correct word.
Write the words in complete sentences in your book.

a. It is not (right / tight) to (fight / fright) with your friend.
b. The plane flew (why / high) into the sky.
c. The man drove the car too fast down the (runway / highway).
d. Please do not (frighten / brighten) the little kittens.
e. There are many mountains in the (lowlands / highlands).
f. The thief shone the (bright / sooty) torch in the dark room.
g. The plane flew up (bright / high) in the sky.
h. I need to turn on the (light / knight) to read my book.

**RHYME time** › Copy this rhyme into your book and then ...

1. Circle six words that end in '**–ight**'.
2. Underline two words that end with '**–s**'.
3. Draw a square around two words that are written in capital letters.

*You've no need to light a nightlight,*
*On a light night like tonight.*
*For a nightlight's light is slight,*
*And tonight's a night that's light.*
*When a night's light, like tonight's light,*
*It is really not quite right*
*To light nightlights with their slight lights*
*On a light night like tonight.*

*And don't take flight on a quiet night,*
*On a quiet night like tonight.*
*For a quiet night's flight might*
*Show you that night flights,*
*even slight flights,*
*On quiet nights are fright nights.*
*So if you take flight, fly on bright nights,*
*For a bright night's flight's alright.*
*GOODNIGHT!*

# WORD KNOWLEDGE › Past, present and future tense verbs

**RULE**

Remember, a **verb** is an action word that tells us what someone or something is doing.
Verbs change to show us **when** someone or something is doing an action.
If something happened **in the past**, we use the **past tense** of the verb, for example: *I jumped up high.*
If something happens **in the present**, we use the **present tense** of the verb, for example: *I jump high* OR *I am jumping high.*
If something will happen **in the future**, we use the **future tense** of the verb, for example: *I will jump high.*

**1** Copy this table into your book.
Complete it with verbs to show that things are happening in the past, present or future.

| Past | Present | Future |
|---|---|---|
| ran | run | will run |
| stopped | | |
| played | | |
| sat | | will sit |
| crawled | | |

**2** Write a sentence for each group of words in your book.

**a.** ate I eat I will eat

**b.** kick I kicked I will kick

## COMMON WORDS ›

**1** Choose words from the Spelling List to fill the gaps.
Write the complete sentences in your book.

**a.** My dad has to go to _ _ _ _ at 6am.
**b.** The big dog _ _ _ _ _ _ _ _ _ _ the small cat.
**c.** The old woman performed a _ _ _ _ _ trick.
**d.** I saw _ _ _ _ _ _ _ with a mud mask.
**e.** There are ten people _ _ _ _ _ _ to my party.

**2** The word '**someone**' is made from two smaller words: '**some**' and '**one**'.
Write three more words in your book that begin with the word '**some**'.

Weekly Spelling List to be tested at the end of the week

**Spelling LIST**

loved
magic
work
coming
someone
right
frightened
highway
lighting
high

**Writing activity › When Something Bad Happened**

- Write about a time in the past when something really painful or bad happened to you. Don't forget to tell what happened, where it happened and how you felt.

## FOCUS > 'er' sound (as in 'her'/'third'/'fur'/'early'/'worm')

**1** Choose a word from the Word List for each picture.
Write the words in alphabetical order in your book.

f__ __n

ch__ __p

sh__ __t

b__ __n

b__ __glar

t__ __tle

**2** Write five of the complete words in sentences in your book.

**3** Find words from the Word List that have a similar meaning to these words.
Write the words in the word frames. The first one has been done for you.

a. 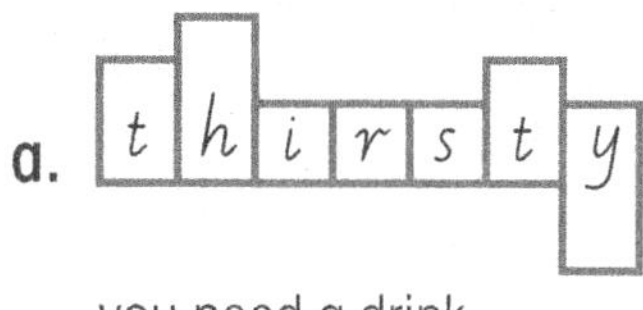

you need a drink

b. 
a thief or a robber

c. 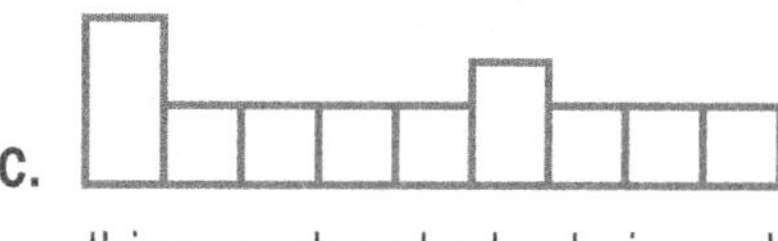
things such as beds, chairs and tables in houses

d. 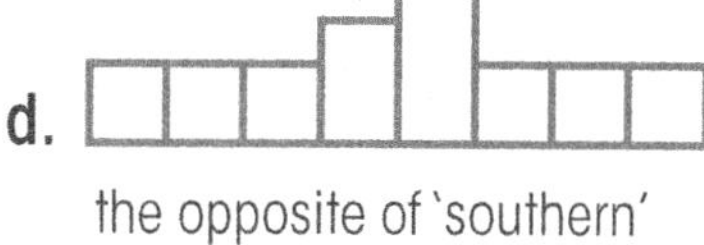
the opposite of 'southern'

e. 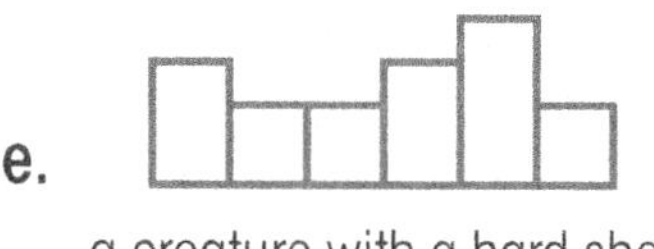
a creature with a hard shell

f. □□□□□
someone who cares for sick people

**4** Copy these proverbs into your book.
Underline words with the letters that make the '**er**' sound.

a. The early bird catches the worm → *The early bird catches the worm.*
b. First come, first served.
c. One good turn deserves another.
d. A bird in the hand is worth two in the bush.
e. Practise makes perfect.
f. Actions speak louder than words.

**Word LIST**

first
fern
church
bird
birth
herb
person
turn
burn
chirp
western
northern
eastern
southern
return
turtle
purple
thirsty
under
perfume
further
furniture
birthday
shirt
nurse
burglar
early
earth
earn
earthquake
worm
worth
word

**5** Choose words from the Word List to complete these sentences. Write the complete sentences in your book.

a. We go to _ _ _ _ _ _ _ every Sunday.
b. The girl's _ _ _ _ _ _ _ _ smelt like flowers.
c. Everyone celebrated the _ _ _ _ _ of the new baby girl.
d. You could hear the birds _ _ _ _ _ _ from a long way off.
e. The man's face went _ _ _ _ _ _ _ when he swallowed the fly.
f. The big, tall truck could not get _ _ _ _ _ the bridge.

**6** Write as many words as you can in your book, using the magic word machines.

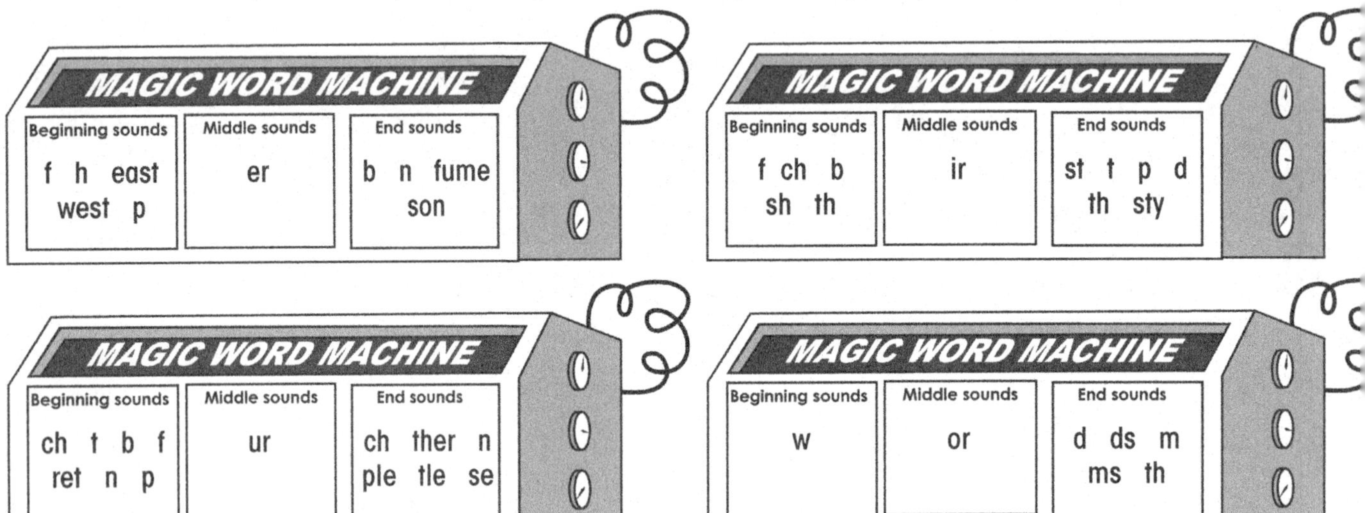


**7** Sort these words into groups that have the same letter patterns, for example: summ<u>er</u>, sist<u>er</u>, butt<u>er</u>.

| | | | | |
|---|---|---|---|---|
| summer | butter | reverse | number | certain |
| sister | river | turtle | fir | every |
| church | winter | letter | chirp | girth |
| skirt | herb | nurse | turn | thirty |
| dirty | water | paper | expert | furnish |
| thunder | burnt | stir | finger | circus |

**8** Choose the correct word. Write the words in complete sentences in your book.

a. I put the wood on the fire so that it would (burn / turn).
b. We had to go (further / burglar) into the bush to find the cuscus.
c. Leti tore her new (purple / skirt) on a thorn.
d. Michael is the (egg / person) who saw the thief take the car.
e. It is important to (return / turn) the tools to the farmer.
f. Are you going any (further / father) along the road?
g. It is my (birthday / breakfast) next month.

# WORD KNOWLEDGE > Noun suffixes

**RULE**

A **suffix** is added to the end of a word.
Some suffixes are added to **verbs** to form **nouns**, for example: *dance – dancer*.
The verb is 'dance' and the suffix is '**–er**'. Adding the suffix forms the noun 'dancer'.

**1** Read these words about people who do different jobs.
Copy them into your book and then choose a word from the Noun Suffix Box to match each job.

**a.** someone who teaches
**b.** someone who runs
**c.** someone who fixes pipes
**d.** someone who sells meat
**e.** someone who mines underground
**f.** someone who swims
**g.** someone who writes for a newspaper
**h.** someone who bakes bread
**i.** someone who dances
**j.** someone who builds houses

**Noun Suffix BOX**

builder
baker
plumber
dancer
miner
reporter
teacher
runner
butcher
swimmer

**2** Copy this rhyme into your book.

**a.** Circle the nouns with the '**–or**' suffix.
**b.** Underline the noun with the '**–ier**' suffix.
**c.** Put a cross next to the word with the '**–ar**' suffix.

*Tinker, tailor,*
*Soldier, sailor,*
*Rich man, poor man,*
*Beggar man, thief!*

# COMMON WORDS >

**1** Choose words from the Spelling List to fill the gaps.
Write the complete sentences in your book.

**a.** I would like to be in the football _ _ _ _ today.
**b.** I am _ _ _ _ _ _ very sleepy when I wake up in the morning.
**c.** Did you see that strange _ _ _ _ _ flying through the air?
**d.** The _ _ _ _ hit the reef and sank quickly.
**e.** I went through the _ _ _ _ and into the next room.

Weekly Spelling List to be tested at the end of the week

**2** Write these three words in sentences in your book.

always already almost

**Spelling LIST**

team
thing
always
boat
door
furniture
nurse
person
birth
first

**Writing activity > When I Grow Up**

■ When you grow up, what would you prefer to be – a tinker, a tailor, a soldier, a sailor, a rich man, a poor man, a beggar, a thief or something else altogether? Write about what job you hope to do when you are an adult and the reasons why you would like to do that job.

## FOCUS > 'w' sound (as in 'water' / 'what')

**Word LIST**

| | |
|---|---|
| will | whisker |
| win | wasp |
| wheat | window |
| wheel | wolf |
| wag | whisper |
| whale | whirlwin |
| wed | wash |
| well | witch |
| wind | way |
| whip | would |
| wood | wigwam |
| where | weak |
| why | wore |
| what | worm |
| when | wear |
| web | waste |
| wife | weight |
| whistle | wail |
| wheeze | wizard |

**1** Choose the letters 'w' or 'wh' to fill the gaps in these words from the Word List. Write the complete words in your book.

| | | | | |
|---|---|---|---|---|
| __ __eel | __ __ale | __eb | __ __istle | __ __irl__ind |
| __olf | __indow | __ed | __ig__am | __ail |

**2** Write five of the complete words in sentences in your book.

**3** Find rhyming words for these words. Write each pair of words in your book.

go red freeze there sty bell thistle
tale life bin good pitch paste

**4** Choose words from the Word List to complete these sentences. Write the complete sentences in your book.

a. Ouch! I have been stung by a __ __ __ __!
b. The __ __ __ __ __ of the cart fell off when it hit a rock.
c. The __ __ __ __ __ __ made a magic potion.
d. The teacher closed the __ __ __ __ __ __ to stop the rain coming in.
e. If you eat all that ice cream you are going to put on __ __ __ __ __ __.
f. The men __ __ __ __ masks at the sing sing.

**5** Use a 'wh–' word from the Word List to complete these riddles. Write the complete riddle (including the question and answer) in your book.

**Q.** _______ would a baby ape sleep? → **A.** In an apricot.
**Q.** _______ can't a bicycle stand by itself? → **A.** Because it's two tyred.
**Q.** _______ was the teacher cross-eyed? → **A.** Because she couldn't control her pupils.
**Q.** _______ would a baby chick say if it saw an orange in its nest? → **A.** Look at the orange marmalade.
**Q.** _______ did one tonsil say to the other? → **A.** Let's get dressed, the doctor's coming to take us out.

**! Challenge**

- Can you write a riddle of your own that begins with 'What', 'Why' or 'Where'?

## 6

Write as many words as you can in your book, using the magic word machines.
Write the words in your book under the correct heading:

a. 'w–' words

b. 'wh–' words

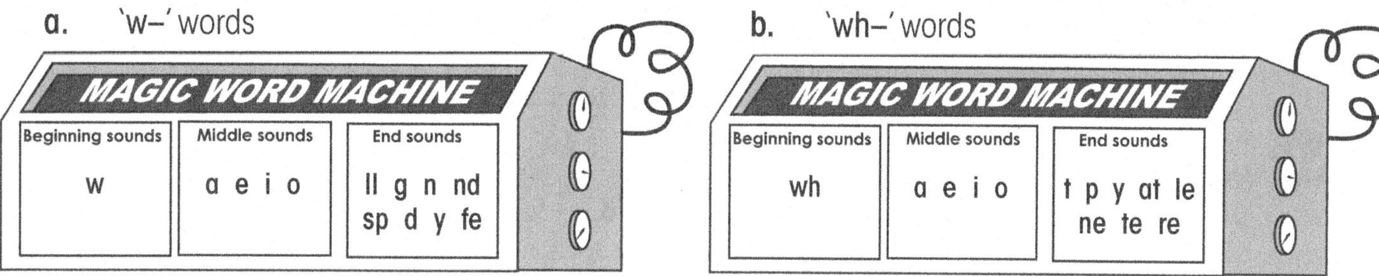


## 7

Change one letter in each word to fill the gap and make a new word.
Write the new words in your book in alphabetical order. The first one has been done for you.

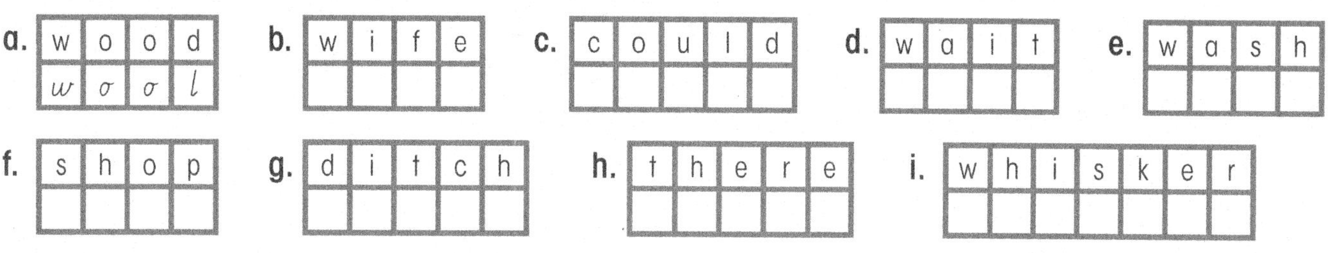


## 8

Copy these words into your book. Circle the odd one out and write it in a sentence.

| | | | | | |
|---|---|---|---|---|---|
| a. | win | wig | wit | will | quit |
| b. | what | when | why | how | where |
| c. | whip | wheel | wig | wheat | when |
| d. | whenever | whatever | forever | wherever | |
| e. | wood | will | wag | wigwam | quicksand |
| f. | wasp | bee | wallaby | wolf | wombat |

## 9

Copy this crossword in your book. Write the correct word for each clue and find the mystery word.
Write the mystery word in a sentence in your book.

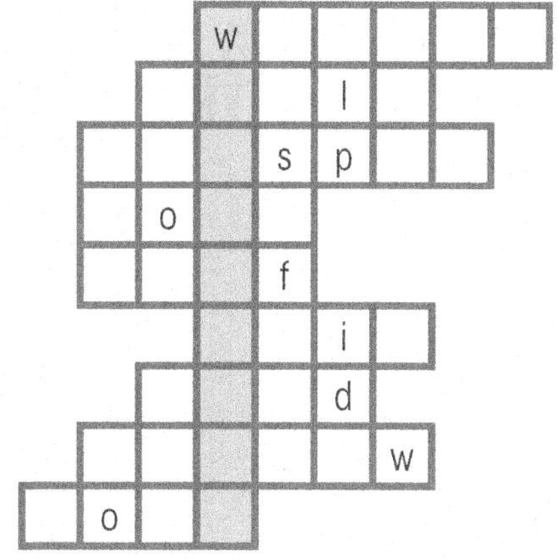


... cars, bikes and buses have these
... the largest mammal in the sea
... to speak very quietly
... a long wriggly creature
... a wild animal like a big dog
... a lion tamer cracks this
... air moving about quickly
... a glass pane that you see through
... a material that burns on a fire

# WORD KNOWLEDGE > Alliteration

**RULE**

**Alliteration** is when several words in one sentence begin with the same letter.
For example: *The wicked witch whistled into the wind.*

**1** Copy this poem into your book.
Underline all the words that begin with the letter '**w**'.

***Clouds***
*White sheep, white sheep*
*On a blue hill.*
*When the wind stops*
*You all stand still.*
*When the wind blows*
*You walk away slow.*
*White sheep, white sheep,*
*Where do you go?*
*by Christina G. Rossetti*

**2** Complete these sentences in your book using alliteration.

a. Seven shiny sharks ________.
b. Ten tiny toddlers ________.
c. Four fantastic ________.
d. Six silly ________.

## COMMON WORDS >

**1** Choose words from the Spelling List to fill the gaps.
Write the complete sentences in your book.

a. The cat curled _ _ _ tail right around its body.
b. The _ _ _ _ _ _ _ _ wore a crown of sparkling diamonds.
c. I hope we can go _ _ _ _ _ _ _ _ at the market tomorrow
d. Our _ _ _ _ _ _ _ was very pleased with our work today.
e. Simon wanted to stay out _ _ _ _ _ the sun went down.

**2** Choose the words in the Spelling List that begin with '**wh–**'.
Write them in sentences in your book.

Weekly Spelling List to be tested at the end of the week

**Spelling LIST**

teacher
its
princess
shopping
until
whisper
where
worm
wife
when

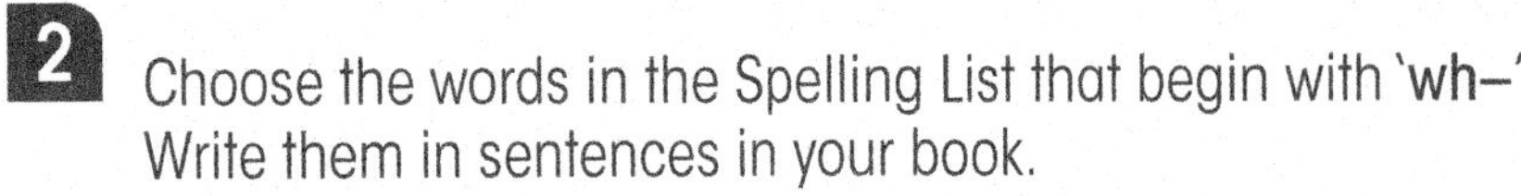

**Writing activity > Big Trouble**

- Write about a time when you got into big trouble.
In your recount, describe where you were, when it happened, what happened and why you got into so much trouble.

# FOCUS › 'qu' sound (as in 'queen'/'squeal')

**1** Choose the letters '**qu**' or '**squ**' to fill the gaps in these words from the Word List. Write the words in your book.

| | | | |
|---|---|---|---|
| __ __een | __ __ __are | __ __ __eal | __ __estion |
| __ __eer | __ __ __eak | __ __ __elch | __ __ __eeze |
| __ __intuplets | earth__ __ake | | |

**2** Write five of the complete words in sentences in your book.

**3** Find words from the Word List that have a similar meaning to these words. Write the words in the word frames. The first one has been done for you.

a. q u i c k

fast

b.

a tiny noise a mouse makes

c. 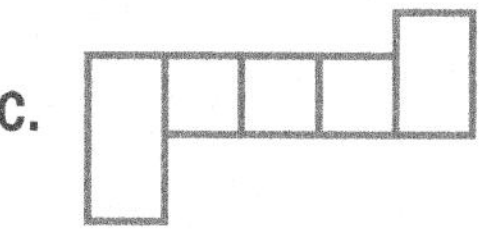

not noisy

d. 

to hold very tightly

e. 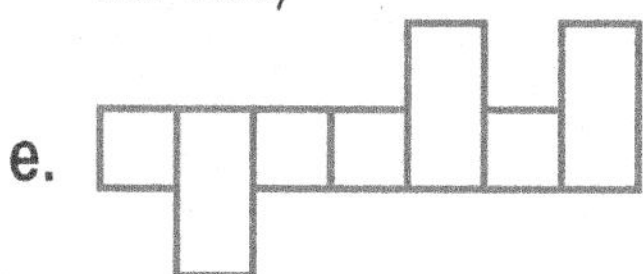

the sound you make when you tread in mud

f. 

a shape with four equal sides

**Word LIST**

quick
quack
squeeze
squeal
queen
squaw
quad
squad
quin
quintuplets
squid
squelch
quit
square
squint
quiz
quilt
earthquake
question
quite
quiet
quarter
squeak

The word 'quadruplets' means four of a kind and the word 'quintuplets' means five of a kind. These are long words and can be difficult to spell, so it is easier if you break them into parts. For example: quad / rup / lets, quin / tup / lets.

**4** Write these words in your book.
Break them into parts and write the parts in your book.

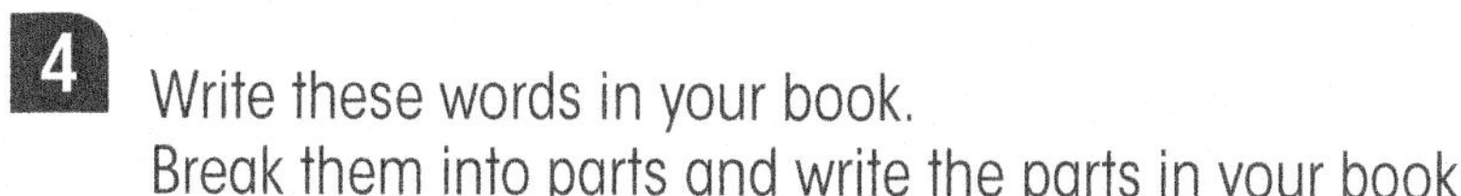

handkerchief cupboard hamburger roundabout
earthquake toothbrushes quickly

**HINT**
You can use a dictionary to help you.

**5** Find the difference in meaning between 'quiet' and 'quite'.
Write each word in a sentence in your book to show its meaning.

**6** Write as many words as you can in your book, using the magic word machine.

**MAGIC WORD MACHINE**

| Beginning sounds | Middle sounds | End sounds |
|---|---|---|
| qu squ | a e i o | ck al te en d it n t z eze tuplets ruplets |

**7** Choose words from the Word List to complete these sentences.
Write the complete sentences in your book.

a. If you _ _ _ _ _ _ _ the fruit it will bruise.
b. The teacher asked a _ _ _ _ _ _ _ _ that I could not answer.
c. The pig let out a big _ _ _ _ _ _ _ when the boy pulled its tail.
d. Leti's mother said, "There's too much noise, so please be _ _ _ _ _."
e. The king and _ _ _ _ _ _ _ came to visit our village yesterday.
f. When I look at the book I have to _ _ _ _ _ _ _ to see the words.

**8** Copy these words into your book.
Circle the odd one out and write it in a sentence.

| | | | | | |
|---|---|---|---|---|---|
| a. | quiz | quick | quad | kick | quiet |
| b. | squelch | squeak | speak | squid | squeal |
| c. | quads | quadruplets | quintuplets | triplets | quins |
| d. | quiet | quieter | quietly | cute | quietest |

**9** Copy this crossword in your book. Write the correct word for each clue and find the mystery word.
Write the mystery word in a sentence in your book.

... what sound does a duck make?
... what is the king's wife called?
... what shape has four equal sides?
... what sound does a mouse make?
... what is the opposite of loud?
... what is the opposite of slow?
... what is the opposite of answer?
... what is short for quintuplets?

# WORD KNOWLEDGE > Onomatopoeia

**RULE**

**Onomatopoeia** means that the sound the word makes matches its meaning.
For example: *splash, boom, tick tock, screech, plop.*

**1** The sound of these '**qu–**' words matches their meaning. Write each one in a sentence in your book.

squelch squeak quack squawk squeal

**2** Copy this table into your book and fill in the gaps. The first one has been done for you.

| Sound | What makes the sound |
|---|---|
| buzz | bee |
| tick tock | |
| plip plop | |
| quack | |
| chirp | |
| hiss | |
| roar | |
| moo | |

# COMMON WORDS >

**1** Choose words from the Spelling List to fill the gaps. Write the complete sentences in your book.

a. We are going to the swimming _ _ _ _ tomorrow.
b. All the _ _ _ _ _ _ _ were locked in the cage.
c. The _ _ _ _ _ galloped away.
d. I was not _ _ _ _ so I stayed home.
e. I saw the boy _ _ _ _ the book from the shop.

**2** Find four '**qui–**' words and three '**squ–**' words.

Weekly Spelling List to be tested at the end of the week

**Spelling LIST**

pool
take
well
animals
horse
quick
quarter
square
squeeze
quit

**Writing activity**

- Would you like to be a king or queen?
- Write about why it might be good and why it might not be so good.

Revision

# FOCUS > 'igh', 'er' sounds

**1** Choose the letters '**igh**' or '**ight**' to fill the gaps in these words from Word Bank ①. Write the words in your book.

| | | | |
|---|---|---|---|
| s__ __ __ | n__ __ __ __ | fl__ __ __ __ | r__ __ __ __ |
| h__ __ __way | h__ __ __lands | l__ __ __ __ | br__ __ __ __ |
| h__ __ __ | sunl__ __ __ __ | fr__ __ __ __ened | fortn__ __ __ __ |

**2** Write all the words from Word Bank ① that begin with the letter '**h**' in sentences in your book.

**RULE**

Remember, a **homophone** is a word with the same sound as another word, but with different spelling and a different meaning, for example: *right* and *write.*

**3** Choose 'right' or 'write' to fill the gaps. Write the complete sentences in your book.

**a.** My teacher is always __________.
**b.** You should always do the __________ thing.
**c.** I will __________ you a note.
**d.** Stay on the __________ side of the road.
**e.** If you are late, your mother must __________ me a letter.
**f.** Can you __________ the letters of the alphabet backwards?

**4** Choose the letters '**ur**', '**er**', '**ir**' or '**or**' to fill the gaps in these words from Word Bank ②. Write the words in your book.

| | | | |
|---|---|---|---|
| b__ __n | t__ __tle | ch__ __ch | b__ __th |
| ch__ __p | sh__ __t | th__ __d | b__ __glar |
| th__ __st | p__ __fume | west__ __n | w__ __rth |

**5** One word from Word Bank ② has not been used. Write it in a sentence in your book.

**6** Find rhyming words from Word Bank ② for these words. Write each pair of words in your book.

third perch burp turn burst

**Word BANK ①**

highway
sigh
night
highlands
flight
bright
high
sunlight
right
fortnight
frightened
light

**Word BANK ②**

church
thirst
bird
burn
chirp
turtle
burglar
perfume
shirt
western
birth
third
worth

# FOCUS › 'w', 'q' sounds

**1** Choose the letters '**w**' or '**wh**' to fill the gaps in these words from Word Bank ③. Write the words in your book.

| | | | |
|---|---|---|---|
| __ __y | __in | __eak | __ed |
| __ood | __ __istle | __eight | __ __irl__ind |
| __ __eelchair | __eb | __ednesday | |

**2** Write these words in sentences to show the different meanings.

where / wear    would / wood    wring / ring
whale / wail    witch / which    way / weigh

**3** Write two questions in your book for each of these question words.

what  why  when

**4** Find rhyming words from Word Bank ③ for these words. Write each pair of words in your book.

thistle  fed  feat  beak  pail  pin  sky

**5** Choose the letters '**qu–**' or '**squ–**' to fill the gaps in these words from Word Bank ④. Write the words in your book.

| | | | | |
|---|---|---|---|---|
| __ __ick | __ __ __ __eak | __ __intuplet | __ __een | __ __arter |
| __ __ilt | earth__ __ake | __ __ __are | __ __ __id | __ __it |

**6** Write these words in sentences to show the different meanings.

quiet  quite

**7** Find rhyming words from Word Bank ④ for these words. Write each pair of words in your book.

whizz  reporter  trick  whack  green  knit

**Word BANK ③**

why
win
weak
Wednesday
whistle
wood
wail
wed
wheat
whirlwind
weight
web
wheelchair

**Word BANK ④**

quintuplet
squid
quiz
earthquake
quit
square
quarter
squeak
quack
quilt
queen
quick

# Blast off!

## How to play

Throw a dice to move a step.
Then say a word that begins with the consonant blend you land on.
If you can't say a word, miss a turn.
The first player to 'blast off' is the winner.

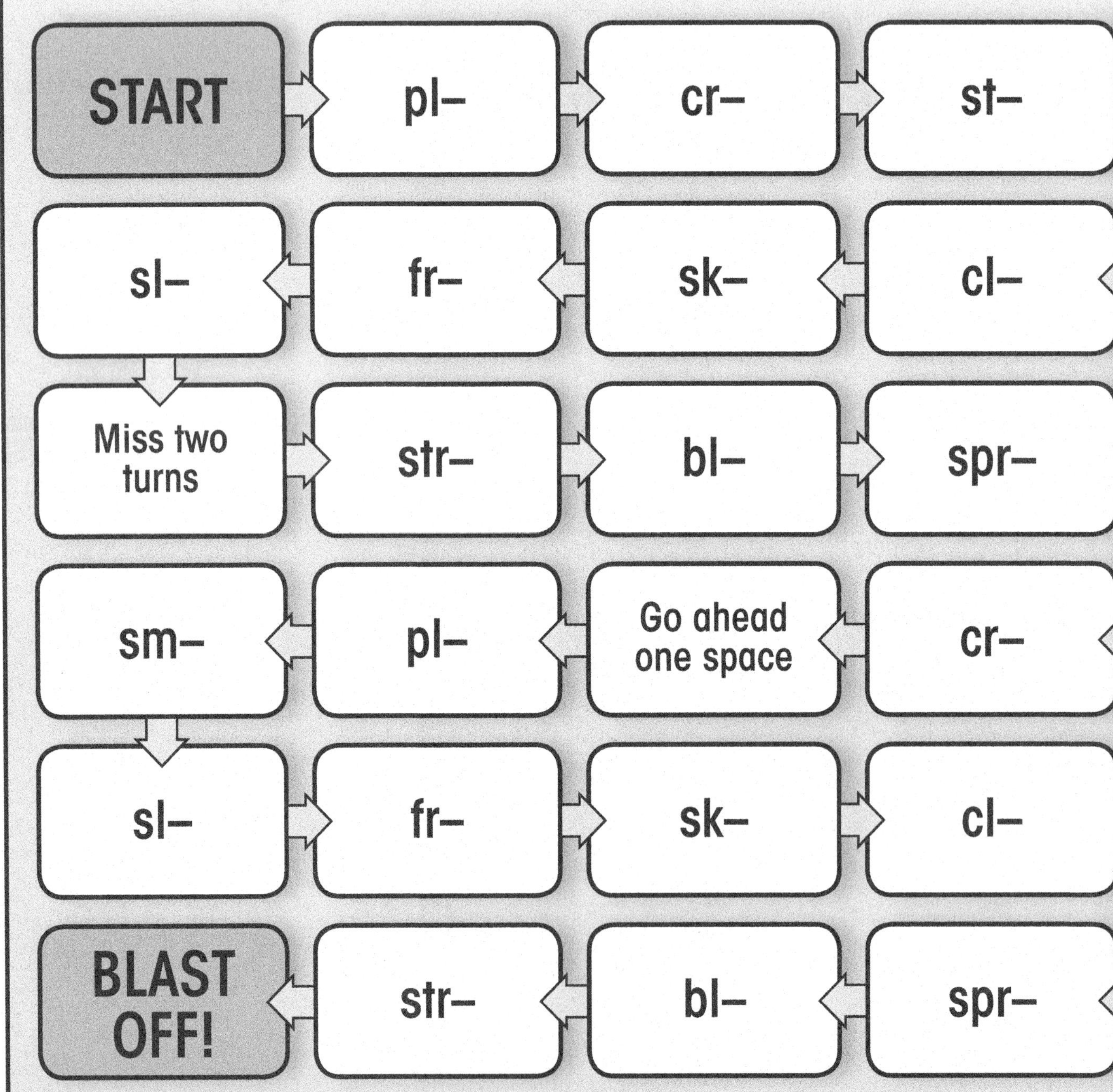

| | | | |
|---|---|---|---|
| fr– | Go back to start | pr– | sw– |
| gr– | Miss a turn | sn– | gl– |
| Go ahead three spaces | tr– | sp– | br– |
| st– | fl– | pr– | sw– |
| gr– | sn– | gl– | Miss a turn |
| cr– | sk– | st– | br– |

# Words in words!

## How to play

Throw a dice to move a step.
Then say a small word inside the word you land on, for example: boxer – box.
If you can't say a word, miss a turn.
The first player to reach the finish is the winner.

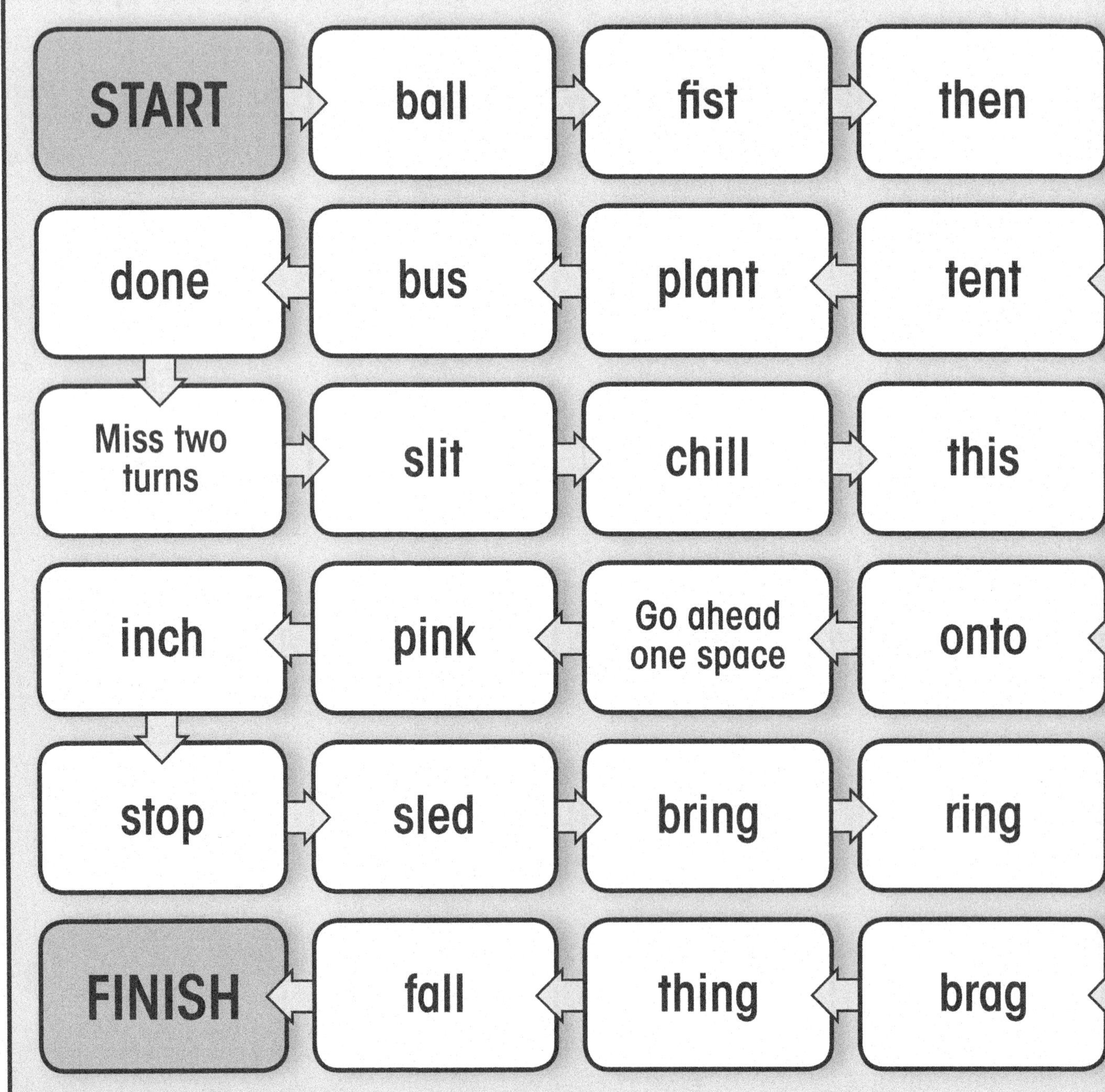

| | | | |
|---|---|---|---|
| that | Go back to start | must | call |
| wins | Miss a turn | cold | slip |
| Go ahead three spaces | list | candy | meat |
| fond | mend | upset | fit |
| hold | slap | fast | Miss a turn |
| ball | spring | garden | finger |

# Answers

## Unit 1

1 ship, brush, wash, fish, sheep, crash, shout, shell
3 wish, shine, sheep, shout, shell, fish
5 Many answers, for example: ship, shone, sheep, shop, crashes, bushes, dishes, sashes, fish, wash, crush, flash
6 flashing, shut, brush, shock, wash, shell

### WORD KNOWLEDGE ›

1 cup / board, tooth / brush, birth / day, dish / washer, ear / ring
2 suntan, sundial, sunshade, sunstroke, sunspot, sunburn, sunlight, sunset, sunglasses, sunshine, sunbake, sunscreen

### COMMON WORDS ›

1 **a** took; **b** other; **c** good; **d** about; **e** party
2 shut, fish, crashes, shout, dishes

## Unit 2

1 thumb, moth, teeth, thin, north, mouth, bath, birthday
3 thin, teeth, thirty, mother, thistle, south, birthday
5 Many answers, for example: thank, thick, thumb, thorn, brother, mouthful, gather, bath, south, mouth, north
6 tooth, both, moth, thank, thirty, thumb, bother

### WORD KNOWLEDGE ›

1 January, February, March, April, May, June, July, August, September, October, November, December
2 Monday, Tuesday, Wednesday, Thursday, Friday, Saturday, Sunday

### COMMON WORDS ›

1 **a** people; **b** put; **c** friend; **d** didn't; **e** their
2 their, thick, thin, bath, mother, birthday

## Unit 3

1 fish, feet, elephant, giraffe, foal, football, roof, phone
3 **a** six; **b** grunt; **c** next; **d** coffee; **e** photo
4 fat, puff, elephant, foal, phone
5 toffee / coffee, ball / fall, huff / puff, your / four, race / face, goal / foal, thirst / first, tire / fire, turf / surf, stiff / sniff, meet / feet, bone / phone
7 Many answers, for example: sniff, stiff, puff, fluff, gruff, bluff
8 Many answers, for example: fish, fell, fog, fury, feet, foot
9 **a** Friday; **b** coffee; **c** huff, puff; **d** giraffe; **e** sniff; **f** fat

### WORD KNOWLEDGE ›

1 **a** sea; **b** too; **c** knows; **d** some; **e** flower; **f** cheap; **g** knot; **h** meat
2 **a** meet / meat; **b** blue / blew; **c** caught / court; **d** right / write

### COMMON WORDS ›

1 **a** over; **b** see; **c** us; **d** girl; **e** boy, girl
2 fourth, fifth, sixth, seventh, eighth, ninth

## Unit 4

1 chick, chips, patch, witch, children, beach, lunch, hatch
3 **a** dinner; **b** blotch; **c** slip; **d** clip; **e** cats
4 peach, branch, sketch, cheek, chain
7 **a** children; **b** scratched; **c** crutches; **d** stitch; **e** bunch; **f** chain
8 children

### WORD KNOWLEDGE›

1 Mon, Tues, Wed, Thur, Fri, Sat, Sun
2 photograph / photo, refrigerator / fridge, football / footy, telephone / phone, advertisement / ad, January / Jan

### COMMON WORDS ›

1 **a** your; **b** off; **c** dinner; **d** three; **e** likes

## Unit 5 REVISION

**FOCUS ›** 'sh', 'th', 'f', 'ch' sounds

3 **a** thirsty; **b** catch; **c** dishwasher, dishes; **d** photo; **e** itch, scratch; **f** tooth
4 children, witch, sniff, elephant, thunder, father, shut, shout, crush
5 rush / us, rash / ash / as, pea / each, flash / lash / lashes / ash / ashes / as / he, child, chick, ash / as, wish / is
6 **a** feet; **b** giraffe; **c** flag; **d** phone; **e** face; **f** surf
7 **a** chop; **b** pitch; **c** surf; **d** fish; **e** television; **f** shut
8 **a** wash; **b** thick; **c** thong; **d** fish; **e** surf; **f** hatch; **g** peach

## Unit 6

3 **a** spade; **b** race; **c** ape; **d** flames; **e** scrape; **f** space
4 Many answers, for example: mate, lake, dame, gate, gape, cave, game, shave, wave, sat
5 sale, save, scale, scrape, shade, shape, shave, spade, stage, stale
6 **a** made; **b** gate; **c** game; **d** wage; **e** shade; **f** cake
8 behave

### WORD KNOWLEDGE ›

1 they're, it's, you're, can't, I'm, hadn't
2 she is, here is, is not, they are, we are, he is

### COMMON WORDS ›

1 **a** gave; **b** down; **c** water; **d** from; **e** found
2 took / gave, lost / found, up / down, sleep / wake

## Unit 7

3 Many answers, for example: rise, hide, kite, mice, wife, bite, tide, dice, wipe, pipe
4 **a** ice; **b** price; **c** bite; **d** bike; **e** ripe; **f** hike
5 bike, bite, bride, ice, kite, nine, smile, swine
7 ripe, wise, bride, bite, dine, swine, glide, pipe
8 seaside

## WORD KNOWLEDGE ›

1 fox, boy, chicken, fence, shed, house, bucket, dog

## COMMON WORDS ›

1 **a** won; **b** happy; **c** morning; **d** playing; **e** want
2 unhappy / happy, narrow / wide, dislike / like, frown / smile

## Unit 8

3 Many answers, for example: joke, vote, done, doze, phone, home, smoke, slope
4 bone, hose, nose, phone, rope, rose, smoke, throne
5 choke, cope, doze, gnome, note, slope, smoke, spoke, stroke, those, throne
6 **a** poke; **b** throne; **c** spoke; **d** rope; **e** stone; **f** rose
7 **a** telephone; **b** telescope; **c** microphone; **d** microscope; **e** stethoscope; **f** periscope; **g** cyclone; **h** xylophone
9 **a** hope; **b** note; **c** mope; **d** code

## WORD KNOWLEDGE ›

1 villages, girls, tigers, books
2 foxes, brushes, witches, sandwiches
3 singular and plural are the same

## COMMON WORDS ›

1 **a** what; **b** again; **c** love; **d** if; **e** as
2 **a** froze; **b** again; **c** slope; **d** home; **e** love

## Unit 9

3 fumes, flute, pollute, June, nude, parachute
4 **a** fuse; **b** excuse; **c** rule; **d** tube; **e** tune; **f** parachute
5 **a** July; **b** flute; **c** pool; **d** smoke; **e** shoot
6 Many answers, for example: tube, fuse, cute, nude, pollute, include, accuse, crude, salute
7 cut, rude, fuse / us, use / us, muse / us, us, tub
8 parachute

## WORD KNOWLEDGE ›

1 cities, hobbies, spies, ponies, raspberries, stories, puppies, factories
2 parties, navies, countries, babies

## COMMON WORDS ›

1 **a** really; **b** could; **c** shop; **d** game; **e** would
2 tame / game, dune / tune, should / could, chop / shop, refuse / amuse

## Unit 10 REVISION

Long vowels a-e, i-e

1 flame, page, guide, quite, kite, grime, made, stage, slime, cave, grade, bride, fade, nine, wife, stroke
3 **a** broke; **b** dive; **c** bride; **d** gave; **e** ride, bike; **f** whale; **g** like, ripe
4 spade, outside, bike, tame, flame, swine, whale, crime, wise

Long vowels o-e, u-e

1 froze, stone, rude, gnome, envelope, joke, smoke, cute, amuse, brute, fuse, June, vote, cone, parachute
3 **a** fumes; **b** chose; **c** tune, flute; **d** home; **e** stone, broke; **f** rude; **g** salute
4 stone, mule, antelope, rose, parachute, confuse, nose, dune, gnome

## Unit 11

1 street, stream, seat, asleep, wheel, dream, scream, speed, wheat, lead, steep, feet / feat
3 peek / peak, leak / leek, flee / flea, meat / meet, feet / feat, reel / real, cheap / cheep, weak / week, creak / creek, team / teem
4 Possible answers include: **a** sweet; **b** deep; **c** weed; **d** creak; **e** dream; **f** real; **g** steam; **h** beast
5 Many answers, for example: keep, creek, green, deep, creak, meal, lean, dream
7 **a** feed; **b** weed; **c** clean; **d** sweep; **e** creek; **f** meet, street; **g** jeep; **h** sleep

## WORD KNOWLEDGE ›

1 cold / chilly, weep / cry, fast / swift, huge / big, shiny / bright, torn / ripped, dirty / filthy, tiny / small
2 **a** large; **b** quiet; **c** laugh; **d** walk

## COMMON WORDS ›

1 **a** down; **b** found; **c** water; **d** gave; **e** went
2 bee, knee

## Unit 12

1 grow, toasted, soak, also, coach, tomorrow, yellow, pillow, boast, rainbow, groan, own, nobody, ghost, hello
3 Possible answers include: **a** throw; **b** yellow; **c** most; **d** toasted; **e** pillow; **f** coach; **g** arrow
4 Many answers; for example: window, low, grow, crow, willow, road, coat, foam, soap
6 low, rain / bow / in, no / body, grow / own, blow / wing / in, toast / as

## WORD KNOWLEDGE ›

1 first / last, big / little, up / down, hot / cold, on / off, strong / weak, happy / sad, light / dark, clean / dirty
2 cold, empty, lost, weak, late, big
3 thin, short, right, shut, rough, light

## COMMON WORDS ›

1 **a** food; **b** baby; **c** watch; **d** by; **e** named
2 know, ghost
3 rainbow, nobody, slowcoach

## Unit 13

1 stew, due / dew, value, clue, avenue, screw, untrue, drew, corkscrew, jewel, statue, knew
3 statue, jewel, corkscrew, untrue, avenue, screwdriver
4 **a** blew; **b** glue; **c** stew; **d** blew; **e** true; **f** new; **g** screw
5 Many answers; for example: new, chew, screw, knew, avenue, due, rescue, queue
7 **a** rescue; **b** grew; **c** clue; **d** dew; **e** queue; **f** view; **g** new

## WORD KNOWLEDGE ›

1 house / brick, tomato / ripe, star / bright, baby / tiny, hair / curly, cat / fluffy, day / sunny, giraffe / tall
2 fast, big, hungry, big black, happy, little

## COMMON WORDS ›

1 **a** outside; **b** away; **c** family; **d** favourite; **e** has
2 cork / screw / crew / or; screw / crew / drive / driver / river

## Unit 14

1 sky, find, unkind, dragonfly, behind, sly, July, by, climb, grind, multiply, mind, butterfly, child, cry, bicycle

3 Possible answers include: **a** mind; **b** dry; **c** unwind; **d** my; **e** kind; **f** wild

4 **a** child; **b** grandchild; **c** dry; **d** blind; **e** multiply

5 Many answers; for example: child, riot, wind, trial, find, drying, cry, July

6 be / hind / in, kind / in, grand / and / child / an, butter / but / fly, dragon / drag / on / fly / rag, cry / in, fin / in

7 **a** climb; **b** behind; **c** fry; **d** find; **e** unkind; **f** July; **g** trial

### WORD KNOWLEDGE ›

3 curly, brown, smiley, blue, leather, tall, long, loud, best

### COMMON WORDS ›

1 **a** lunch; **b** shops; **c** man; **d** looked; **e** football

2 unkind, unwind

3 climb

## Unit 15 REVISION

**FOCUS ›** 'e', 'o' sounds

3 reading, steaming, speeding, leading, speaking

4 scream, screamed, seat, sheep, speak, speed, steam, stream

7 towed, boasted, owned, glowed, snowed

**FOCUS ›** 'u', 'i' sounds

3 stewing, chewing, viewing, screwing

4 screw, screwdriver, screwed, statue, stew, stewing

6 **a** behind; **b** my; **c** try; **d** butterfly; **e** blind; **f** multiply

7 behind, blind, find, grind, kind, mind, unkind, unwind

## Unit 16

1 stray, tail, pay, strain, maid, pail, brain, stray, rain, snail, sail, hay

2 **a** train, rails; **b** snail; **c** play, day; **d** trail, way; **e** spray, stain; **f** rain; **g** stay; **h** paid

3 Possible answers include: **a** pray; **b** stain; **c** bail; **d** spray; **e** sail; **f** play; **g** plain; **h** pray

4 rain / in, main / in, be / bet / tray / ray, sail / ail, rail / ail / way, chain / in

6 **a** grain; **b** braid **c** frail; **d** stray; **e** plain

### WORD KNOWLEDGE ›

1 **a** sing; **b** hop; **c** cut; **d** threw;

2 **a** walked; **b** talked; **c** walked; **d** played; **e** turned

### COMMON WORDS ›

1 **a** wanted; **b** lost; **c** playground; **d** paint; **e** try

2 playground

3 play/ lay / ground / round

## Unit 17

1 beer, year, near, dear / deer, sear, peer, queer, clear, rear

2 **a** deer; **b** clear; **c** spear; **d** beer; **e** year; **f** cheer; **g** engineer; **h** near

3 Possible answers include: **a** dear, deer; **b** career, cheer; **c** steer, tear; **d** smear, shear

4 sap / appear / pear / is / ear, cheer / ring / in, spear / red / pear / ear, tear / drop / ear, near / by / ear, fear / ear

5 spear, shear, ear, steer, beer, deer, cheer, dear, queer

6 **a** dear; **b** volunteer; **c** sheer; **d** rear; **e** year; **f** hear, near

7 **a** cheering , steering; **b** sneered, steered; **c** career, disappear; **d** year, tear; **e** gears, fears

### WORD KNOWLEDGE ›

1 **a** swinging; **b** balancing; **c** cracking; **d** jumping; **e** driving; **f** watching; **g** cutting; **h** shooting

### COMMON WORDS ›

1 **a** cousin; **b** fairy; **c** games; **d** Friday; **e** stayed

2 career, cheering, cousin, fairy, Friday, games, stayed, steered, tear, year

## Unit 18

1 baby, happy, puppy, party, honey, valley, monkey, hungry, carry, pretty, lady, alley

2 **a** honey; **b** very; **c** pretty, party; **d** chimney; **e** parsley; **f** hurry; **g** jockey

3 Possible answers include: **a** monkey, many; **b** party, alley; **c** dirty, donkey; **d** baby, body; **e** trolley, tiny; **f** money, many; **g** twenty, turkey; **h** funny, forty

4 tin / in, him, went, fun, read, part / art, man / an, store / ore

5 pretty, pony, hurry, turkey, jockey, angry, twenty, monkey, puppy

6 **a** baby / very; **b** donkey; **c** hungry; **d** cheeky; **e** journey; **f** money

### WORD KNOWLEDGE ›

1 **a** loudly; **b** quietly; **c** slowly; **d** angrily

3 **a** gently; **b** loudly; **c** quickly; **d** quietly; **e** clearly

### COMMON WORDS ›

1 **a** woke; **b** come; **c** ever; **d** ball; **e** old

2 ten, twenty, thirty, forty, fifty, sixty, seventy, eighty, ninety, one hundred

## Unit 19

1 saw, shawl, form, corn, report, crawl, paw, horse, yawn, horn, law, north

2 **a** north; **b** pawpaw; **c** brawl; **d** hawk; **e** torch; **f** dawn; **g** draw; **h** morning

3 Possible answers include: **a** shawl, seesaw; **b** sort, sport, stork; **c** crawl, flaw, caw; **d** storm, scorn, morning; **e** prawn, pawn, north; **f** report, sort, port; **g** force, fawn, north

4 fort, north, corn, prawn, fork, brawl, pawpaw, horse, report

5 **a** shawl; **b** warn; **c** yawn; **d** shorn; **e** short; **f** fawn

6 **a** storm, form; **b** pork, cork; **c** brawled, crawled; **d** yawn, dawn; **e** short, snort; **f** brawl, crawl

### WORD KNOWLEDGE ›

1 **a** noisily; **b** silently; **c** quickly; **d** slowly; **e** smoothly; **f** loudly

### COMMON WORDS ›

1 **a** scared; **b** room; **c** who; **d** new; **e** nice

2 cork, morning, new, nice, pawpaw, report, room, scared, seesaw, who

## Unit 20 REVISION

**FOCUS ›** 'a', 'eer' sounds

2 sprain, spray, Spain

5 steer, sneer, shear, sheer, smear, spear

7 **a** hear; **b** jeer; **c** giraffe; **d** queue; **e** spring; **f** eye

**FOCUS ›** 'y', 'or' sounds

**2 and 4** everything, everyone, everywhere

6 strawberry, storming, storm

8 **a** plenty; **b** alley; **c** ten; **d** nearby

9 pawpaw, port, prawn

## Unit 21

1 ground, sow, round, now, spout, amount, allow, loud, pouch, count, cow, wow
2 **a** account; **b** how; **c** cow; **d** crouch; **e** ground; **f** allow; **g** shout; **h** discount
3 **a** count; **b** spout; **c** somehow; **d** wound; **e** allow; **f** eyebrow
4 am / mount, loud, back / ground / round, some / so / me / how, round, any / how / an
5 shout, cow, hound, sound, cloud, prowl, pouch, bound
6 **a** ground; **b** now; **c** account; **d** crouched; **e** somehow; **f** couch
7 **a** eyebrow, bound; **b** grouch, growl; **c** shout, how; **d** cow, couch; **e** account, allow; **f** count, clouds

### WORD KNOWLEDGE ›

1 **a** he; **b** she; **c** they; **d** his; **e** it
2 **a** she, her; **b** I, it, you; **c** you, her; **d** they, it, his; **e** we

### COMMON WORDS ›

1 **a** inside; **b** cake; **c** best; **d** tree; **e** it's

## Unit 22

1 ploy, joint, boil, loin, spoil, decoy, avoid, point, join, enjoy, toy, joy
2 **a** avoid; **b** joy; **c** employ; **d** boil; **e** alloy; **f** annoy; **g** toil; **h** groin
3 **a** avoid; **b** decoy; **c** sirloin; **d** loin; **e** convoy; **f** employ
4 boy, spoil / oil / led, joy, join / in, oil / so, hoist / is
5 coil, spoil, soil, sirloin, ploy, coin, annoy, boy
6 **a** appoint; **b** destroy; **c** convoy; **d** ahoy; **e** hoist; **f** rejoin; **g** employ; **h** cowboy
7 **a** hoist, toy; **b** schoolboy, boil; **c** avoid, joy; **d** destroy, annoy; **e** coin, moist; **f** sirloin, soil

### WORD KNOWLEDGE›

1 **a** barked; **b** ate; **c** turn; **d** rode; **e** played; **f** catch

### COMMON WORDS ›

1 **a** long; **b** fell; **c** how; **d** movie; **e** soccer
2 cowboy

## Unit 23

1 blare, air, flare / flair, chair, hare / hair, repair, spare, unfair, square, stare / stair, pair / pare, dare
2 **a** chair; **b** mare; **c** beware; **d** spare; **e** funfair; **f** hardware; **g** aware; **h** lair
4 Many answers, for example: repair, chair, pair, stare, beware, square
5 stare, scare, air, pair, blare, share, nightmare, airport
6 **a** hair; **b** pair; **c** stare; **d** fare; **e** prepare; **f** dare

### WORD KNOWLEDGE ›

1 **a** because; **b** but; **c** and; **d** so; **e** before; **f** so

### COMMON WORDS ›

1 **a** last; **b** sleep; **c** also; **d** swimming; **e** know
2 bare, square
3 air, chair, dairy

## Unit 24

1 bath, calm, glass, pass, plaster, party, banana, class, shark, car, smart
2 **a** starfish; **b** plaster; **c** tomato; **d** mask; **e** palm **f** harm; **g** bath; **h** father
3 fast, tomato, halves, smart, class, calf, car, father
4 star / tart / art, ask / as, ark, bask / ask / ball / as, pass / port / sport / or, star / tar / fish / is, part / art / par, spark / ark / par
5 **a** past; **b** calm; **c** glass, path; **d** flask; **e** park; **f** calf
6 Possible answers include:
   **a** basketball, banana, last;
   **b** farmyard, fast, dart;
   **c** plaster, path, start;
   **d** charm, class, mark
7 **a** car, far; **b** art, part; **c** park, spark; **d** calm, palm; **e** father, rather; **f** glass, pass

### WORD KNOWLEDGE ›

1 **a** on; **b** up; **c** along; **d** beside; **e** off

### COMMON WORDS ›

1 **a** told; **b** don't; **c** just; **d** yes; **e** around
2 calm, palm

## Unit 25 REVISION

### FOCUS › 'ou', 'oy' sounds

1 sound, anyhow, amount, wow, cow, scout, prowl, allow, count, aloud, somehow, pound
3 **a** cloud; **b** round; **c** punch; **d** scout
4 allow, aloud, amount, anyhow, cloud, count, cow, eyebrow, pound, prowl, round, scout, scowl, somehow, sound, wow
5 choice, cowboy, joint, boiling, voice, join, toy, void, point, annoy, joy, coin, avoid, destroy, tomboy, schoolboy
8 **a** scout; **b** found; **c** boiling; **d** annoying

### FOCUS › 'air', 'ar' sounds

3 air, aware, airport, airway, armchair
5 shark, tomato, calm, calf, basketball, half, glass, carport, park, for, mask, flask, spark, palm, ask
7 **a** fare; **b** coin; **c** glasshouse; **d** cats; **e** potato
8 ask, basketball, calf, calm, carport, far, flask, glass, half, mask, palm, park, shark, spark, starfish, tomato

## Unit 26

1 **a** same; **b** track; **c** lack; **d** snag; **e** sand; **f** every
2 tuck / luck / struck / stuck, above, dust / rush, uncle, front, welcome, mother, dust, glove
3 **a** love; **b** bunch; **c** front; **d** done; **e** brother; **f** truck; **g** bump; **h** mother; **i** must; **j** hunt, gun
4 mud, front, mother, bunt
5 **a** mother; **b** struck; **c** above; **d** hunch; **e** come; **f** must
6 **a** fun; **b** come; **c** rust; **d** love; **e** undone; **f** outcome
7 broth / rot / her, bun, love, moth / other / her, truck, shun / hunt, undo / done / one / on, hug, one / on, stun, tuck

### COMMON WORDS ›

1 **a** beach; **b** finished; **c** killed; **d** today; **e** funny
2 someone, anyone
3 some / one / on, any / one / on / an

## Unit 27

1 **a** hand; **b** keep; **c** lad; **d** scant; **e** bunt; **f** never
2 tent, bread / head / spread / ready / thread / dread / tread / ahead / overhead / headache / headdress / headlight / headmaster / headphone, dread / dress / headdress, spent / spend, yell / yellow, headdress, spread, slept / sled

3 **a** tread; **b** feather; **c** yellow; **d** slept; **e** melt; **f** scent; **g** pencil; **h** weather, tent
4 headache, bent, pencil, yellow, leather
5 **a** ahead; **b** headlight; **c** headmaster; **d** bend; **e** pen, pencil; **f** hen, yellow; **g** headdress
6 **a** leather; **b** overhead; **c** bread; **d** headache; **e** fret; **f** spread
7 head / he, yell / low, sun / set, read, cent, pen, head / dress / address, head / phone / one / he / on

### WORD KNOWLEDGE ›

I'll never get this homework done!
I'm clever – I can do the splits!
Stop that now!
Ouch!

### COMMON WORDS ›

1 **a** headache; **b** yesterday; **c** book; **d** computer; **e** near
2 headdress, headlight, headmaster, headache, headphone

## Unit 28

1 swan, washing, wasp, hospital, what, hole, comic, cross, hot, lock, swallow, robber, was, holiday, bottom
2 **a** wash; **b** bottom; **c** moth; **d** boss, cross; **e** holiday; **f** robber; **g** what; **h** swallow
3 block, wallet, robber, swan / swallow, copy, rocket, wallaby, knot / knock, squabble / squash
4 **a** same; **b** packet; **c** sick; **d** class; **e** when; **f** roof
5 **a** lock; **b** squabble; **c** wallaby; **d** squash; **e** copy; **f** hole; **g** wash; **h** knot
6 **a** hot; **b** swan; **c** boss; **d** what; **e** was; **f** bottle
7 **a** wasp, wallet; **b** rocket, robber; **c** bottle, bottom; **d** holiday, dog; **e** hot, hog; **f** squash, swan

### WORD KNOWLEDGE ›

1 **a** at the bananas; **b** flew into the tree; **c** swam away; **d** crowed very loudly; **e** flew the plane; **f** is our minister

### COMMON WORDS ›

1 **a** help; **b** castle; **c** zoo; **d** now; **e** ride
2 knock, knot

## Unit 29

1 chicken, cricket, fifty, gymnastics, insect, window
2 prison, quickly, gypsy, Egypt, river, wrist, hymn / gymnastics / gymnasium, mystery, fifty
3 **a** sister; **b** prison; **c** pyjamas; **d** picnic; **e** window; **f** what; **g** gym; **h** chicken
4 **a** happy; **b** hikes; **c** gentle; **d** cycle; **e** forty; **f** tribe
5 **a** bit; **b** hymn; **c** spill; **d** quiz; **e** insect; **f** wrist; **g** gym; **h** window
6 **a** river; **b** kitchen; **c** fifty; **d** hit; **e** quickly; **f** silly
7 **a** spill, silly; **b** stick, sixty; **c** prison, pyjamas; **d** chicken, cricket; **e** fifty, sixty; **f** quickly, sit

### WORD KNOWLEDGE ›

1 **a** Dad said, "I want my dinner."
**b** Mum said, "It's time for bed."
**c** The train driver shouted, "All aboard!"
**d** Simon cried, "Give that back!"

### COMMON WORDS ›

1 **a** toy; **b** tried; **c** cousins; **d** more; **e** look
3 gymnastics, gymnasium

## Unit 30 REVISION

**FOCUS › 'u', 'e' sounds**

3 snug, some, someone, struck, sun
5 jetting: wetting, setting, betting, letting, getting; bread: dread, spread, thread, head, dead, tread; send: bend, spend, lend, dead-end, mend, send, blend

**FOCUS › 'o', 'i' sounds**

1 swan, wand, tossed, mop, dog, strong, pot, cross, watch, wash, long, often
3 wand, wander, want, was, wash, wasn't, watched
4 top / bottom, colder / hotter, coldest / hottest, found / lost, weak / strong, weaker / stronger, hard / soft, shorter / longer, short / long
5 middle, little, city, gym, riddle, gypsy, fill, hill, spill, myth
7 silly, sister, sixty, spill, symbol, synonym
8 stupid / silly, fast / quickly, jail / prison, cold / chilly, puzzle / quiz, stream / river, opposite / antonym, similar / synonym, slap / hit

## Unit 31

1 king, clown, kite, kangaroo, kidnap, ticket, camel, clock, camp, comb, sock, lock, koala, cabbage, kelp
3 **b** lucky; **c** kidnap; **d** kettle; **e** cricket; **f** stockings
6 Many answers, for example: cat, coast, come, could, kid, kelp, keep, brick, stuck, track, sock
7 **a** kilogram; **b** checked; **c** capital; **d** kitchen; **e** pocket
8 **a** keep; **b** country; **c** kidnap; **d** trike
9 cricketer

### WORD KNOWLEDGE ›

1 **a** "How are you?"
**b** "Look at that."
**c** "Not now."
**d** "Come over here."
**e** "Get it quickly!"
**f** "Wait a minute."
2 **a** "I fell off the wall," cried the boy.
**b** "Someone ate the chocolate," said Dad.
**c** "Kick it through the goal posts," shouted the coach.
**d** "Stay in after school," said the teacher.
**e** "I can't find my pen," wailed the child.
**f** John said, "I have lost my wallet."
**g** The little boy cried, "I want my mummy."

### COMMON WORDS ›

1 **a** happily; **b** I'm; **c** four; **d** started; **e** find
2 calm, com**b**, cas**t**le

## Unit 32

1 jet, jelly, jug, jigsaw, giraffe, giant, magician, vegetables, cage, June, gypsy, jewels
2 go, get, angry, grab, grunt; stranger, angel, danger, giant, magic
3 giraffe, giant, cage, page, voyage, magic, gypsy, Germany, ginger, gym, vegetables, garage, cabbage, magician, stranger, danger, angel; jam, jab, jet, jug, jazz, jelly, joke, June, July, jewels, jetty, jacket, jigsaw, jumper, jawbone, January, joy
6 **a** jewels; **b** cage; **c** magician; **d** vegetables; **e** giraffe; **f** jewels; **g** jigsaw

7 **a** garage; **b** January; **c** jawbone; **d** giant; **e** jigsaw; **f** voyage

8 **a** jelly, jazz, joke, joy
**b** angel, danger, giant
**c** jacket, jockey, jumper
**d** ginger, gym, magician
**e** page, cage, garage, stage

9 **a** cousin; **b** games; **c** August; **d** fruit; **e** clown

10 vegetable

## WORD KNOWLEDGE >

1 **a** reindeer; **b** aircraft; **c** salmon; **d** sheep; **e** fish

## COMMON WORDS >

1 **a** rabbit; **b** dragon; **c** five; **d** much; **e** turned

2 rabbit, giraffe, jelly, cabbage, jetty

3 giraffe, cabbage, magic

## Unit 33

1 sun, fence, centipede, palace, soap, sandwich, bicycle, seventy, police, sent / cent

2 cent, centipede, cycle, celery, circus; cat, cycle, cub, clap, count, circus, cross

3 circle, palace, cent, cycle, rice, fence, nice, place, circus, celery, centipede, twice, parcel, police, cement, piece, decide, voice, bicycle, mice; sun, six, sale, sang, somebody, sometime, circus, soap, sent, seventy, Saturday, sandwich, silly, silent

6 **a** rice; **b** centipede; **c** nice; **d** police; **e** cycle

7 **a** soap; **b** seventy; **c** palace; **d** sang; **e** sandwich

8 **a** fence, palace, celery, sun;
**b** bicycle, police, rice, twice;
**c** silent, silly, Saturday, sang;
**d** cement, nice, cycle, sale;
**e** decide, voice, soap, parcel

9 **a** danger; **b** jigsaw; **c** nowhere; **d** jacket; **e** motorcar

10 policeman

## WORD KNOWLEDGE >

1 **a** kicked; **b** told; **c** drove; **d** galloped

2 **a** is coming; **b** has lost; **c** is building; **d** will be coming; **e** will be leaving

## COMMON WORDS >

1 **a** make; **b** chips; **c** cousins; **d** another; **e** breakfast

## Unit 34

1 zebra, prison, tigers, apples, zip, present, quiz, zoo, zero

2 span, sad, story, stop, song, start, salt; tigers, nose, apples, rulers, papers, chisel, zoo

3 as, is, busy, prison, present, chisel, resident, rose, president, rulers, papers, apples, has, tigers, nose, chasm; zoo, zip, whiz, zoom, zero, dizzy, zebra, zipper, zigzag, zap, zinc, zest, zone, sizzle, zucchini, lazy, buzz

5 **a** zebra; **b** zipper; **c** nose; **d** prison; **e** lazy

6 **a** buzz; **b** rulers; **c** sizzle; **d** present; **e** zebra

7 **a** busy, president, sizzle, tigers
**b** zigzag, zinc, quiz, prison
**c** buzz, chasm, zap, chisel, zoom
**d** zoom, present, zone
**e** zip, chisel, president, dizzy

8 zigzag

## WORD KNOWLEDGE >

2 boy / friend, mouse / trap, bed /room, school / boy, rail / way, water / fall, farm / yard, girl / friend, paint / brush, wheel / chair

## COMMON WORDS >

1 **a** walk; **b** great; **c** together; **d** present; **e** couldn't

2 present, nose, busy, papers

## Unit 35 REVISION

**FOCUS >** 'c', 'j' sounds

1 clown, kitten, koala, kettle, comb, kite, castle, kiosk, kidney, calf, kiss, kangaroo

2 castle, clown, comb, calf

3 front / back, hot / cold, can / can't, going / coming, could / couldn't, lucky / unlucky, release / capture, kind / unkind, went / came

4 jot, giant, cabbage, magic, gypsy, jetty, vegetable, juggle, jewel, luggage

5 gymnastics, gypsy, vegetables, magic, giant, luggage, cabbage

6 monster / giant, rubbish / junk, soft / gentle, happiness / joy, gemstones / jewels, bug / germ, puzzle / jigsaw, leap / jump, huge / gigantic, trouble / danger

**FOCUS >** 's', 'z' sounds

1 once, sister, sunset, grocer, cycle, circular, seasick, fence, police, place

2 once, grocer, fence, sentence, saucer, cycle, police, circular, place

4 dry / juicy, useful / useless, clever / silly, certain / uncertain, buy / sell, hard / soft, war / peace, take / receive, well / sick

5 sizzle, whizz, zipper, zucchini, zebra, chosen, chisel, busy, present, quiz

6 present, busy, chisel, prayers, chosen

7 snout / nose, nought / zero, hum / buzz, fastener / zip, jail / prison, test / quiz, active / busy, wildlife park / zoo, gift / present

## Unit 36

1 fright, high, highway, knight, light, sigh

2 **b** tight; **c** highlands; **d** high; **e** frighten; **f** highway; **g** bright

3 **a** right; **b** might; **c** night / light; **d** bright; **e** sigh

5 Many answers, for example: highway, tighten, frighten, bright

6 **a** bite; **b** lowland; **c** time; **d** wrong

7 **a** right, fight; **b** high; **c** highway; **d** frighten; **e** highlands; **f** bright; **g** high; **h** light

## WORD KNOWLEDGE >

1 ran, run, will run; stopped, stop, will stop; played, play, will play; sat, sit, sill sit; crawled, crawl, will crawl

## COMMON WORDS >

1 **a** work; **b** frightened; **c** magic; **d** someone; **e** coming

## Unit 37

1 burglar, burn, cheep, fern, shirt, turtle

3 **a** thirsty; **b** burglar; **c** furniture; **d** northern; **e** turtle; **f** nurse

4 **a** The early bird catches the worm.
**b** First come, first served.
**c** One good turn deserves another.
**d** A bird in the hand is worth two in the bush.
**e** Practise makes perfect.
**f** Actions speak louder than words.

5 **a** church; **b** perfume; **c** birth; **d** chirp; **e** purple; **f** further

6 Many answers, for example: perfume, eastern, person, chirp, shirt, thirsty, church, burn, purple

7 summer, sister, thunder, butter, river, winter, water, reverse, herb, letter, paper, number, expert, finger, certain, every; church, burnt, turtle, nurse, turn, furnish; skirt, dirty, stir, fir, chirp, girth, thirty, circus
8 **a** burn; **b** further; **c** skirt; **d** person; **e** return; **f** further; **g** birthday

## WORD KNOWLEDGE ›

1 **a** teacher; **b** runner; **c** plumber; **d** butcher; **e** miner; **f** swimmer; **g** reporter; **h** baker; **i** dancer; **j** builder
2 **a** tailor, sailor; **b** soldier; **c** beggar

## COMMON WORDS ›

1 **a** team; **b** always; **c** thing; **d** boat; **e** door

# Unit 38

1 wheel, whale, web, whistle, whirlwind, wolf, window, wed, wigwam, wail
4 **a** wasp; **b** wheel; **c** witch; **d** window; **e** weight; **f** wore
5 Where; Why; Why; What; What
6 Many answers, for example: wand, wed, wind, won, what, whey, white, whole
8 **a** quit; **b** how; **c** wig; **d** forever; **e** quicksand; **f** bee
9 whirlwind

## WORD KNOWLEDGE ›

1 white, when, wind, walk, where

## COMMON WORDS ›

1 **a** its; **b** princess; **c** shopping; **d** teacher; **e** until
2 whisper, where, when, where

# Unit 39

1 queen, square, squeal, question, queer, squeak, squelch, squeeze, quintuplets, earthquake
3 **a** quick; **b** squeak; **c** quiet; **d** squeeze; **e** squelch; **f** square
4 hand/ker/chief, cup/board, ham/burg/er, round/a/bout, earth/quake, tooth/brush/es, quick/ly
6 Many answers, for example: quite, queen, squat, squeeze
7 **a** squeeze; **b** question; **c** squeal; **d** quiet; **e** queen; **f** squint
8 **a** kick; **b** speak; **c** triplets; **d** cute
9 question

## WORD KNOWLEDGE ›

2 buzz/ bee, tick tock / clock, plip plop / rain, quack / duck, chirp / bird, hiss / snake, roar / lion, moo / cow

## COMMON WORDS ›

1 **a** pool; **b** animals; **c** horse; **d** well; **e** take
2 Many answers, for example: quiet, quilt, quip, quiz, squad, square, squid

# Unit 40 REVISION

**FOCUS ›** 'igh', 'er' sounds

1 sigh, night, flight, right, highway, highlands, light, bright, high, sunlight, frightened, fortnight
2 highway, highlands, high
3 **a** right; **b** right; **c** write; **d** right; **e** write; **f** write
4 burn, turtle, church, birth, chirp, shirt, third, burglar, thirst, perfume, western, worth
5 bird
6 third / bird, perch / church, burp / chirp, turn / burn, burst / thirst

**FOCUS ›** 'w', 'q' sounds

1 why, win, weak, wed, wood, whistle, weight, whirlwind, wheelchair, web, Wednesday
4 thistle / whistle, fed / wed, feat / wheat, beak / weak, pail / wail, pin / win, sky / why
5 quick, squeak, quintuplet, queen, quarter, quilt, earthquake, square, squid, quit
7 whizz / quiz, reporter / quarter, trick / quick, whack / quack, green / queen, knit / quit